MULTICULTURAL FOUNDATIONS OF PSYCHOLOGY AND COUNSELING

Series Editors: Allen E. Ivey and Derald Wing Sue

Healing the Soul Wound:
Counseling with American Indians and Other Native Peoples
Eduardo Duran

Counseling and Psychotherapy with Arabs and Muslims:
A Culturally Sensitive Approach
Marwan Dwairy

Learning from My Mother's Voice:
Family Legend and the Chinese American Experience
Jean Lau Chin

Community Genograms:
Using Individual, Family, and Cultural Narratives with Clients
Sandra A. Rigazio-DiGilio, Allen E. Ivey,
Kara P. Kunkler-Peck, and Lois T. Grady

Multicultural Encounters:
Case Narratives from a Counseling Practice
Stephen Murphy-Shigematsu

Healing the Soul Wound

COUNSELING WITH AMERICAN INDIANS AND OTHER NATIVE PEOPLES

EDUARDO DURAN

Foreword by Allen E. Ivey

TEACHERS COLLEGE PRESS

Teachers College, Columbia University
New York and London

06-1883

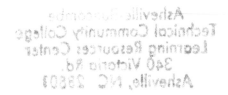
Published by Teachers College Press, 1234 Amsterdam Avenue, New York, NY 10027

Library of Congress Cataloging-in-Publication Data

Duran, Eduardo, 1949–
    Healing the soul wound : counseling with American Indians and other native peoples / Eduardo Duran ; foreword by Allen E. Ivey.
        p. cm. — (Multicultural foundations of psychology and counseling)
    Includes bibliographical references and index.
    ISBN-13: 978-0-8077-4690-5 (cloth : alk. paper)
    ISBN-10: 0-8077-4690-8 (cloth : alk. paper)
    ISBN-13: 978-0-8077-4689-9 (pbk. : alk. paper)
    ISBN-10: 0-8077-4689-4 (pbk. : alk. paper)
        1. Indians of North America—Mental health. 2. Indians of North America—Mental health services. 3. Indians of North America—Psychology. 4. Indians of North America—Counseling of. 5. Psychotherapy. I. Title. II. Series.
    RA448.5.I5D87 2006
    616.89′008997—dc22   2005046666

ISBN-13:   ISBN-10:
978-0-8077-4689-9 (paper)   0-8077-4689-4 (paper)
978-0-8077-4690-5 (cloth)   0-8077-4690-8 (cloth)

Any merit generated by these words
is dedicated toward the liberation from suffering
of all beings in all the realms.

Contents

Foreword

I WAS DEEPLY HONORED when asked to write the Foreword to this important book. Simply put, Eduardo Duran's *Healing the Soul Wound: Counseling with American Indians and Other Native Peoples* is the most innovative and thought-provoking scholarship that I've read in a long time. Duran combines personal experience, scholarship, and wisdom in a profound way. We see many "blurbs" about the wonders of each new book. But Duran's book is something beyond the ordinary. Taken seriously and applied, it represents a paradigm shift that will transform theory and practice.

What can this book do for you, the busy scholar or practitioner? If you are Native American, you are in for a real treat for here you have someone that speaks the truth in a way that will enable you to practice your beliefs in a way different from Traditional empirical approaches, while still using their practical strategies. In addition, you will learn how to bring soul to the therapeutic process and become what Duran terms a "soul healer."

If you are not of Native American origin, this book will be even more important to you. You'll discover a challenging critique of Traditional therapy that, nonetheless, remains respectful of what "is." Like me, you'll have the dualistic Cartesian view of the world challenged. We learn how our culture has wounded not only People of Color, but all of us. In a sense we are all "wounded healers" whose thinking has been colonized by the past history and denial of cultural oppression. We need to see individuals within a historical context that continues to live in the present in the "soul wound," the legacy of intergenerational trauma.

Trauma does not disappear, even with the best cognitive behavioral therapy. It lives on and thrives over time. Survivors of the Native American genocide, the Jewish Holocaust, and African Americans who survived slavery all bear the unconscious marks of the soul wound. Families of traumatized Vietnam veterans or alcoholics, of those who have experienced severe poverty and other challenges, also bear the intergenerational legacy. The ideas that Duran presents here can be used with all these issues and more. Migration and immigration are also forms of trauma experienced by displaced persons. Most U.S. families have dealt with this trauma by denial, but it lives on in mainstream culture in ways that are damaging not only to the individual, but also to society in general. The roots of racism and oppression lie partially in the denial of personal trauma and projection on the Other.

Beyond that, in these pages are invaluable concepts and practical strategies that we can apply directly in our own practice. Duran's case examples represent Native People, but all of them have direct implications for our own work. This is not just a new way of thinking; it is also a culturally specific approach that has profound implications for all counseling and therapy.

You can tell that I'm a believer. I first encountered Eduardo Duran in the pages of the book he co-authored with Bonnie Duran, *Native American Postcolonial Psychology* (1995). That book is now a classic. Taken together, these two books have changed the way I think about counseling and therapy. This new work moves to the next level as it combines exciting theory with highly useful pragmatics of clinical practice. Let us all engage with Eduardo Duran's view of the past, present, and future.

—Allen E. Ivey, Ed.D., ABPP
Distinguished University Professor (Emeritus),
University of Massachusetts, Amherst;
and Professor, University South Florida at Tampa

Acknowledgments

MANY PEOPLE in my life have been a part of this teaching and work throughout my life. The shifting of metaphors in my life has been an ongoing process from early childhood, and countless people have been involved in it. In addition to the people involved in the development of this work, I must acknowledge the spirit of the land that has provided much needed support and guidance.

While I was in graduate school, I was fortunate to meet my spiritual teacher. At the time, I didn't know that he would profoundly crack my cosmic egg and send my way of being in the life-world in a different direction. I offer thanks to Tarrence as he continues to provide support from the spirit-world. I also thank all of my Western teachers who gave me the Western tools that also have provided insight into how the psyche operates.

I thank John Perry, Ronald Teague, Bob Morgan, Carl Jung, Joseph Goldstein, Sabina Lucas, Friedrich Nietzsche, Victor Frankl, Jim Willems, Dreamtime Old Apache Woman, and others who have been helpful in the bridging of ideas from one cultural context to another. Early on, Ron Teague wrote letters to Joseph Campbell and James Hillman to get their insight into the realm that I was entering as I started my work with Native/Aboriginal/Original People. They, along with teachings from Native Elders, provided insight into the idea of the "soul wound," which later became better known as "historical trauma."

As I have done in previous works, I must mention the spirit of Coyote who continues to guide me through treacherous terrain. Without the insight provided by the howl of this Sacred Relation, I would have remained stuck in a life-world with only one metaphor. This would have made my life a lot less interesting. Of course, interesting implies that there is a wider realm of experience and part of that realm encompasses pain as well as joy.

I want to thank Judith Firehammer for her expert editing. Her contribution goes further than simple editing of grammar and such. Her deep understanding of the therapeutic process delineated in these pages has provided an excellent source of validation and bridging of ideas. She truly has brought a new level of cultural competence to this work and consequently to our field. Without her help, this work may not have made much sense to anyone except myself as the author. This would have rendered the work useless. As it stands, the work will be moving into all types of therapeutic and healing environments where it will do the most good.

—Eduardo Duran

Introduction

L IBERATION DISCOURSE involves taking a critical eye to the processes of colonization that have had a deep impact on the identity of
Original Peoples; as a result a new narrative of healing will emerge.
The mental health profession has been instrumental in fostering the colonial ideation of Native Peoples all over the world.[1] I am merely bearing
witness and bringing awareness to this process, to change it. By turning a
critical eye on our professional activities of healing, we liberate ourselves
as well.

It was with some trepidation that I agreed to write the present book. I
had to decide whether I would try to embroider the fabric of the clinical
work with academic language and theoretical constructs or simply say
what needs to be said. In my discussions with Allen Ivey, co-editor of this
book series, he let me know in very certain terms that he would like to see
the "real stuff," whatever that is. This was very challenging to me because
he was asking from his heart and was speaking with the voice of an elder.
I took his request very seriously and struggled with how to do it. I wondered what could happen and how this work would be received. Much of
the clinical work that I have done for 2 decades is an alchemical amalgamation of Western theory and Traditional Aboriginal theory and practice.
As far as I know, there is not much in the literature that encompasses this
type of treatment method. After careful meditation and prayer, I decided
to move ahead with the project, and what follows is the result of an elder
asking for a talk on how to heal the soul wound.

A reasonable question from the logical positivistic mind would be,
"Does this method work and what is the empirical validity of all this?"
Empirical evaluation of this model was conducted at the Oakland Native
American Health Center. The evaluation consisted of qualitative and quan-
titative analysis of clinical charts that spanned 9 years of clinical work. One
of the variables examined was treatment progress, which was measured
by the Global Assessment of Functioning (GAF) scale of the *Diagnostic
and Statistical Manual of Mental Disorders* (DSM-IV; American Psychiatric
Association, 2000). The scale provides a numerical measure of a patient's

level of psychological, social, and occupational functioning, and may be used to monitor the patient's progress in treatment. The evaluation clearly demonstrated improvement in patients' global functioning in response to this treatment model and approach. A video of the research project was made depicting the method used (Ryan, 2002). Video, instead of a traditional journal paper, was used in order to give the community access to the research findings in keeping with the ideology of healing and liberation. Healing and liberation processes are harmonious with social justice, which also results from this method of intervention with communities.

I want to emphasize that the strategies prescribed in this book are not, I repeat not, techniques. The worst case scenario is that beginning, advanced, or master therapists, thinking in a linear fashion, will believe that they simply can replicate the discussed methods and that this will bring the desired outcome. Why can't these methods be used by anyone? The reason is that these methods are part of a holistic approach to being in the life-world. If therapists who do not have a profound spiritual practice of their own attempt to mimic these strategies, they will be disingenuous and offensive to Native patients. Native patients often have a keen eye for charlatans and those who are attempting to "go native."

Therefore, therapists who do not have a fundamental spiritual tradition that they engage in as part of their life are better off referring patients to another therapist or being honest about the extent of their capability. There is nothing wrong with therapists admitting that they engage in colonizing therapies. Honestly letting the patient know of the limitations of such approaches will be quite refreshing and build the therapeutic alliance so that Western therapies can be optimized. In addition, the therapists then can discuss the issues of historical trauma and acknowledge their complicity in being part of the historical perpetrator. This historical honesty will greatly enhance the healing process while utilizing standard therapies.

Again, I thank Allen Ivey for his courage in asking me to write about the "approach" that I utilize in providing treatment to Native People. I was given this knowledge by a holy man in the Native tradition many years ago, and this energy has been evolving in my day-to-day clinical practice. Therefore, the methods described in this work are truly liberating and healing in that they encompass respect of all traditions and worldviews.

A BRIEF LOOK AT THE LITERATURE

The literature abounds with studies, theories, and clinical approaches that are intended for use with clients who are culturally different from

Euro-Americans. With regard to Native Americans specifically, there is also an abundance of literature that is designed to assist clinicians, in their day-to-day work with Native People, to maintain a level of cultural sensitivity (Sue & Sue, 1990). Some of the issues discussed in this book are congruent with some of this literature. I must note that most of the clinical methods I describe in this book, some of which are presented here for the first time in written form, have not been empirically validated. However, I also must note that the ideas and clinical methods discussed were validated by many people in the Native American community; and the manuscript itself actually was validated by hundreds of community people in an oral tradition context. The method of obtaining validation for the manuscript was simple. It was read before Native People gathered for the purpose of healing. After the manuscript had been read and discussed, people voiced their opinions of it, all of which indicated approval of the methods described. Many of the people voicing an opinion were elders who have knowledge of Traditional healing as well as Western ways of being in the life-world. Several hundred people were involved in this process.

Some of the points brought up in the literature dealing with Native Americans are critical, and they also will be discussed in this book. Although the literature citations may appear dated, it is important to note that little has changed in the perception of Native Americans in our field. Ideas discussed in this brief literature review have become classic concepts (the names associated with the classic literature are still respected in Indian country) in the counseling of Native Americans and in the training of counselors. The difference between this book and past literature is that this book will deal with some of the clinical aspects from a purely non-Western perspective by shifting metaphors; this simply means that I try to change the root image or idea from a Western concept to a Native image, as I describe in several places in the book.

The following aspects of counseling Native Americans that are described in some of the cross-cultural literature deserve mention at this point:

- *Degree of assimilation into Western culture*—This should always be considered when working with Native Americans (Lowrey, 1983; Zitgow & Estes, 1981). I discuss some of the ways that this should be done in a clinical setting with minimal intrusion to the patient. Assimilation can be helpful in understanding the problem and possible interventions.
- *Alcoholism*—This is a common issue that needs to be explored with Native Americans (Zitgow & Estes, 1981). A very specific

intervention to address alcoholism will be discussed in this book because this problem persists across the generations and has resulted in great suffering for Native people.

- *Suicide*—The rates of suicide for Native Americans are twice the national average and therefore must be an issue of concern when Native patients are being treated (Shore, 1988). I will discuss some of the methods that I have used in dealing with this serious situation.

- *Counseling relationship issues*—Sue and Sue (1990) discuss how eye contact, discussion of inner feelings, and increased independence from parents may have to be dealt with differently when working with Native Americans. I will discuss how these issues can be worked through while doing intensive therapy with Native People.

- *Counseling methods*—There is controversy regarding the use of client-centered approaches with Native Americans. Some researchers have argued that these methods actually may be counterproductive when working with Native Americans and that nondirective approaches may be more effective (Miller, 1983; Trimble & LaFramboise, 1985). Nondirective approaches are less individualistic and more systemic in nature than are client-centered methods in which the client is central to the intervention. Clinical methods offering yet another point of view regarding client-centered approaches will be explored in this book. The issue of client-centered therapy has been discussed at length in an earlier work (Duran & Duran, 1995).

- *Initial contact, therapeutic relationship, and source of problems*—These critical issues have been discussed by Carolyn Attneave (1982), who is attentive to the first contact and advises that one should be mindful of handshakes and routine gestures. I also deal with the initial contact and make reference to this interaction as part of the acculturation assessment. Attneave asserts that one may not know the answer to some of the client's problems and that the mutual problem-solving process is more important than the solution. One source of problems, according to Attneave, is the patient's relationship with the White world and the impossibility of living a completely Traditional lifestyle. In this book, I delineate how the source of these problems is rooted in historical trauma, which is a relatively new concept.

- *Tribal-specific treatments*—In a more recent book (French, 2002), specific treatments are discussed for four Native American populations: Cherokee, Sioux, Navajo, and Mestizo. Topics addressed include fetal alcohol bibliotherapy, spiritual counseling, and Mexican remedies. French compares cultural traditions and asserts that Traditional Native societies operate from intragroup cooperation, known as the ethos of harmony, versus the competitive ethos found in Western societies. French also discusses how Western methods, unless modified, do not apply to Traditional Native American patients. In the present work, I lend support to French's notion that Western methods need to be modified, but also make the case for replacing some Western methods by Traditional interventions.

THE IMPORTANCE OF CULTURAL COMPETENCE

In this book, I attempt to bring a "cultural experience" to the reader. I am convinced that people who practice healing/therapy in our profession need to have a closer relationship with natural processes that are not defined in the field of psychology. Our psyches are still emerging from basic organic matter, and it is only recently that we have removed ourselves from natural processes, as described by the Cartesian split. Simply stated, we have become alienated from the natural world because we have made the natural world an object that can be perceived as separate from our immediate experience. The work of healing discussed in these pages in no way attempts to take away from orthodox Western therapeutic interventions. In keeping with liberation discourse ideology, this book will provide another approach that has stood the test of time for millennia in many of our Native American communities.

A Bridge Between Western and Traditional Perspectives

The attempt to bridge worldviews is made in this book by shifting root metaphors and bringing awareness to the archetypal nature of the issues that all human beings face as part of being alive. All of the discussions regarding diagnoses and treatment in this book include shifting the modern pathological diagnosis to an understanding that is harmonious with the natural world as perceived by some Native cultures.

For example, all forms of sickness and healing have been delineated into simple categories by anthropologist Frank Clements (1932), who worked extensively with Original Peoples. Although Clements's research is at least 60 years old, these concepts of healing and illness still hold relevance in the Native life-world and are useful in bridging Native concepts with Western understanding of these ideas. These categories include:

- *Object intrusion*—The belief that an object has intruded into the body. The object can invade the body by some random event, or it can be placed there by someone wanting to cause suffering. Therapy for this type of illness is removal of the object by extracting it through cutting, bleeding, or sucking.
- *Loss of soul*—The belief that one's soul has been lost. This can be easily understood as a depersonalization in which the person may have lost contact with reality.
- *Spirit intrusion*—The belief that illness is caused by an outside entity invading the personality. Relevance can be found in the Western concept of multiple personality disorder.
- *Breech of taboo*—Illness due to the guilt caused when an individual violates a societal rule.
- *Sorcery*—Illness that occurs if someone with power willfully inflicts physical, psychological, or spiritual illness on an individual.

Although the ideas presented by Clements in 1932 may seem odd to most modern providers, I am hoping that the therapeutic/healing profession will be able to understand patients' worldviews, their perception of what ails them, and what can make them better. In no way am I implying that the strategies discussed in this book are a panacea or that they should be implemented with all Native patients. Clinical skill of the highest order will be needed to know when and where these strategies can best help a patient. The therapist must have a high level of training within the Western paradigm, as well as an excellent cultural understanding, to utilize these methods effectively.

This work is motivated by a quest for a healing process that includes the healer. In most Western therapeutic settings, the healer is supposed to present herself as a blank screen. Being a blank screen can enhance the perceived objectivity of the events occurring in the healing process, but at the same time it dehumanizes the Healer and the "wounded healer spirit" that is brought into the healing ceremony. Healers who are part of the Traditional system of healing in Original communities do not pretend that they are beyond the frailties of being human. Instead, the community acknowledges their wounding and healing process, which then can provide the bridge of compassion needed in the healing of patients.

Traditional Distinctions

In reading this book, some people may be led to believe that I have engaged in cultural or tribal glossing because I do not make an issue of discriminating between tribal groups. Glossing refers to the assumption that all tribes are exactly the same culturally. Although there are many similarities, there are differences in language, religion, and other aspects of culture that need to be considered when working with Native People. I purposely engage in what may appear as glossing because I believe that one of the most powerful colonial strategies inflicted on Native Peoples has been convincing us that we are so different from one another. Of course, there are tribal variations in the metaphors of healing. In this work, as in my day-to-day clinical work, I use basic root metaphors that bring a common humanity to the clinical situation. Using root metaphors is also consistent with the concept of the collective unconscious (Jung, 1971, 1977, 1988), with which most people are familiar: the theory that human beings are all connected at a collective level of psyche and that this level of psyche is the source of primordial ideas and images of all human beings. The appearance of cultural glossing has never been a problem in my clinical work, and it should not present a problem to readers unless they prefer to believe that we exist separate from one another.

Historical Context

Concern about the issue of tribal glossing makes sense when dealing with the historical context of a given tribe. Clinicians should be aware that most tribes have gone through a horrendous holocaust. Systematic genocide was inflicted on many of the Original People of this hemisphere, and interventions must address the specific trauma to the individual and/ or group that is being treated. It is critical that attention be given to the particular historical context of the tribe that is being dealt with, to avoid this type of tribal glossing. In essence, this book will provide some of the strategies needed to heal the "soul wound," intergenerational trauma, or historical trauma. Basically, these terms have similar meanings. The difference is that the Native idea of historical trauma involves the understanding that the trauma occurred in the soul or spirit. This book does not provide a cure or "end-all" treatment of the "soul wound." Instead, this work delineates a beginning to a long road ahead in the development of theoretical and clinical applications.

This book unfolds by introducing the reader to the concepts of historical trauma and internalized oppression. These are critical concepts that must be understood in order to begin a shift in the mind of both healer and patient. This shift involves understanding the historical context in the presentation of the clinical problem. In subsequent clinical chapters, I guide the reader through treatment processes that require patience and courage as the metaphor of pathology is renamed and treated as a live entity. This renaming or shifting of metaphor is very important in treating Original People because this is still part of much of what is known as Traditional Healing. Traditional Healing exists in many Native communities and consists of using ancient forms of healing that have evolved over thousands of years in our communities. Some of these methods have been in use since before European contact and therefore have a very specific and organic Native root metaphor. Many Original People still consult Healers in their communities as well as Western providers. Knowledge of the way that the Original Healing life-world operates can be of tremendous help to Western healers, as they then can work alongside their Original therapist colleagues.

There has been a great deal of writing, thinking, teaching, and all sorts of activity in the area of cultural competency and working with so-called minority populations. This appears to be innocent enough; after all, the scientific method has convinced many in our field that science based on data is truly objective. I will, however, come out and say it: This is a misrepresentation at best. The appearance of objectivity has some of its roots implanted in racist ideology of the 19th and early 20th centuries and the psychological quest for labeling people of color as genetically inferior (Gould, 1981). Gould's research demonstrates that the earliest attempts to measure human intelligence were also attempts to demonstrate that people of color are inferior. To say it any other way would be contributing to the misrepresentation and suffering of people of color, who continue to be adversely affected by this illusion of objectivity.

Western research loses relevance when imposed on people of color because its "orientation is basically micro-social, concentrating itself almost entirely on personal characteristics of the individual actors in social processes rather than on socio-historical factors" (Sinha, 1984, p. 21). It is critical that research done with Native People also take into account historical factors. Historical factors also must be of primary concern when dealing in purely clinical settings. The task becomes complex when working with Native People because researchers or clinicians must utilize all of their training, in addition to understanding and implementing sociocultural and historical factors.

PREVIOUS TREATMENT AND RESEARCH: METHODS OF OPPRESSION

As professionals who are supposed to be helping and healing, we may take issue with the argument that much of our effort is not intended to help the person or community. In fact, many of our treatment strategies are designed to control people. In his book *Madness and Civilization*, Foucault (1967) explored how the mental health profession is basically a tool of social control. After the church began to fail to control people, because they were gaining access to written material, it became necessary to implement another form of control. The medical profession, including the original doctors of the mind, took up the power to control. The work of these doctors of the mind evolved into the present-day mental health system. Currently, mental health practitioners hold social control. They can give patients new names through the diagnostic process as well as take away a person's freedom without the same right to due process that a criminal in the judicial system may have.

Culturally incompetent research also can be implemented as a tool of social control. Empirical research falls short when applied to communities of color, and one is disappointed by its artificiality, triviality, and lack of relevance to real-life psychological phenomena (Sinha, 1984). Lack of relevance keeps our understanding at a superficial level when in reality a deeper knowing is required. "The methodology of psychological research has to be broadened to make it more relevant for the study of complex social problems facing Third World countries in the process of development" (Sinha, 1984, p. 21). Sinha makes the point that "unimaginative replications of Western research have been decried and called caricature of Western studies" (p. 20). Ongoing misunderstanding between tribes and research entities complicates the possible contributions that could be made by scientific efforts (Villanueva, 2003).

Because clinical practice is rooted in research, it follows that interventions also may fall short of providing help that is relevant to the patient's particular culture. Much of the daily clinical work done by therapists is influenced by stereotypes found in the media and literature. Unfortunately, these representations of Native Americans are not accurate or positive and may bias the therapist's view of the patient. Fortunately, the lack of objectivity caused by this stereotyping process can be remedied through education and training. This is one of the motivations for writing this book. The therapist's insistence on imposing a different worldview on the patient can be understood as a form of violence against the patient's knowledge life-world. This type of violence is known as "epistemic violence" (Spivak, 1990). One of the key purposes of this book is to offer a means to decolonize and liberate the Native life-world in the process of providing culturally competent treatment for emotional, psychological, physical, and spiritual problems. Liberation hopefully will translate into social justice. It is difficult to attain social justice if one is not aware of being oppressed.

In the past, Native patients were not able to understand the true underlying nature of their problems because these problems have been delineated only recently through the study of historical trauma. Through awareness of the infliction of colonial oppression on Original People through systemic mental health diagnostic "naming ceremonies" (see Chapter 2 for definition), the reader may begin to create a new narrative that can become a form of liberation discourse. By raising awareness of the healing process, we will empower individuals and communities to obtain long overdue social justice and healing.

The case material in the clinical chapters of this book is included in an attempt to formally present liberation discourse (speaking in a voice that is decolonized or at least in the process of being decolonized) and thus allow the once colonized to reinvent themselves in a manner that is within their control. Much of the clinical material in the later chapters involves an obvious shifting in metaphor and may cause some therapists or scholars entrenched in linear thought to experience some apprehension. As a result, they may attempt to hide behind the sacred texts of empiricism and other defense mechanisms that allow the linear ego to regain composure. Attempts to "psychologize" the cultural approaches presented will only alienate the reader from people who believe and understand the world in a different manner. Therefore, an openness of mind is needed when different worldviews are being presented to our awareness.

Lack of understanding of the Native epistemological root metaphor (ways of being in the world, including psychological and spiritual worlds) continues to hinder our profession. Historical narcissism (the belief that one's own system of thinking must be used to validate other cultural belief systems) continues to be an issue in the relationship between Original People and those who hold power in the academic and clinical life-world. I use this strong language because the Original person is expected to fully understand the world of the colonizer simply because the colonizer says so. When it comes to making an effort to understand the life-world of the Original person, the colonizer becomes very creative in using defenses to preserve his Cartesian life-world. The intention of this book is to provide a bridge between Western and Traditional Native healing and in this manner bring healing to the historical trauma that all people have suffered at some time in their history.

Aho!! Mi Takuye' Oyacin. All are my relatives.

NOTE

1. The terms *Native American, Original People,* and *Aboriginal* will be used throughout the text. The term *Native American* replaced the older term *American Indian*; it is popular and considered politically correct in most discussions and literature. Many people view themselves as the people who were on this continent originally. Thus, some Native people use the term *Original People*. In other parts of the world, the term *Aboriginal* is used to refer to Original People and is used in the literature of those countries. My purpose in using these different terms is to impress on Native People that, regardless of the colonial identity given in a name, there is a unifying thread of identity for Original People all over the world and these different names have been used as a divisive tool of oppression. Most Native People prefer to call themselves "Human Beings," and the purpose here is to do away with the separation that has been imposed on Native Peoples.

CHAPTER 1

Wounding Seeking Wounding: The Psychology of Internalized Oppression

"The most potent weapon in the hands of the oppressor is the mind of the oppressed" (Steven Biko, 1970).

I HAVE BEEN ASKED many times by people in the Native American community to write a "how-to" book that would complement the philosophical style of the book entitled *Native American Postcolonial Psychology* (Duran & Duran, 1995). The more theoretical approach of that work did not provide a hands-on approach to clinical practice. Presently, there is a great need for new methods of treating Native people for many life problems. This work was written with the hope that it will influence the practice of other therapists who are searching for a different way of doing psychotherapy. In this book, I present pragmatic methods, not theoretical constructs. The concept of postcolonial discourse as presented in the previous book has evolved in this one into the concept and practice of liberation discourse. Liberation discourse provides some of the practical knowledge needed to heal the wounded souls of our people and communities. Liberation discourse therapy is a process that uses Western as well as Traditional Native metaphor so that culturally competent processes may emerge.

LIBERATION PSYCHOLOGY THROUGH HYBRIDISM

This first chapter is an attempt to clarify some of the underlying issues that may be driving the symptoms of Native American patients seeking help. Trauma that is passed from generation to generation and the effects of the trauma on present health and wellness of the individual, family, and community will be discussed. Internalized oppression as a natural by-product of such trauma or wounding also will be explored.

Hybrid is a term that has emerged out of postcolonial thinking and basically means that there can be two or more ways of knowing and this can be a harmonious process. The concept of ideas existing without hierarchy is key to the liberation and healing process. Decolonizing is a process of liberation. In other words, we are going beyond colonizing, because colonizing is a dehumanizing activity. It is important to mention that I believe we must transcend the notion of "cross-cultural," "cultural sensitivity," and other such ideas that have been in vogue for some time in our field. It is critical that we engage in epistemological hybridism (literal translation: being able to think or see the truth in more than one way). Epistemological hybridism takes the actual life-world of the person or group as the core truth that needs to be seen as valid just because it is. There should never be a need to validate this core epistemology or way of knowing by Western empiricism or any other validating tool. To do so is merely a form of neo-colonization that will only add to the problem.

Presently, our profession is moving toward objectifying healing under the guise of "empirically tested therapies." When the profession validates empirically tested therapies only from a Western logical positivistic paradigm, we engage in Western supremacy disguised as perceived scientific objectivity: a very subtle and clever neo-colonialism that will further alienate people and groups at a time when cultural understanding and compassion are greatly needed if we are to heal our society. By operating in a manner that liberates the individual and community, we humanize and restore human dignity just because it is a dignified thing to be human.

Through the creation of liberation discourse, we help the patient address the immediate problem and simultaneously set in motion the act of decolonizing. This culturally competent approach also can be categorized as "liberation psychology." This approach to healing is long overdue in our field. By decolonizing the patient, we also ensure that chronic problems will be prevented in the future. It is important to note that decolonizing does not apply only to Native People or other people of color who have been colonized. So-called mainstream Westerners also may want to decolonize from the collective consumer colonization process that has been imposed on them. Colonization processes affect human beings at a deep soul level, and the intent of this book is to begin a healing process for all of those who want to restore their humanity in a way that is harmonious with natural laws.

In Chapters 3 through 8, I attempt to guide the reader through a complex yet natural process of therapy that has developed from my work with Original People. Familiar ideas such as diagnoses are translated into ideas that will be foreign to some readers. Other readers may think that the discussion is basic and ask why I even bother to present it.

The largest metaphorical leap undoubtedly will be the shift from psychologizing to spiritualizing. In order for the healing process to make sense to Native People, I have changed psychological (soul) metaphors into spiritual (soul) metaphors. *Soul* is in parentheses because I want to alert the reader that Western and Traditional Native root metaphors are not so far apart when viewed in a historical context. More will be said about this later.

Chapters 5 and 6 contain clinical case material that may help the reader to see how a different worldview deals with problems that fall in the category of psychopathology in a Western paradigm. In these chapters, the currently held concepts of mental or psychological disturbances are examined from an Indigenous theoretical and clinical methodology. The result is that the diagnosis and treatment processes move into a different process world through the re-interpretation of content that is used in most healing/therapeutic settings. Simply stated, pathologizing rhetoric is replaced with rhetoric that allows patients to form relationships with their life-world. This includes forming relationships with the source of their pain so that they can make existential sense of what is happening to them. Most Western therapists would call this a simple reframe, and if that helps to make sense of these methods, so be it.

INTERGENERATIONAL TRAUMA: THE SOUL WOUND

As the first task in my clinical career, I was required to perform a needs assessment for a Native American community in central California. I proceeded with the usual surveys and other techniques, which I had learned in a community psychology class. About 2 weeks after the surveys went out into the community, a community health worker returned them—and most of them were blank. When I inquired why they were not completed, I was told, "We thought that you had more manners than that when we hired you. We thought that your grandmother had taught you better than to go asking these kinds of questions."

Completely devastated at this gross cultural incompetence, I proceeded to ask some of the elders what I should do. I was told that I should listen and not talk so much. One elderly woman took me under her wing. Once I was seen with her, people took time to talk to me. A curious description of the issues began to emerge out of the conversations. When asked about the problems in the community, people did not mention the expected symptom-oriented problems. They began to mention ideas such as "spiritual injury, soul sickness, soul wounding, and ancestral hurt."

I proceeded to do the usual literature review, and nowhere in the literature could I find anything related to soul wounding. As a matter of fact, I could not find the word *soul* in connection to providing mental health services. Even as a beginning psychologist, I wondered if I hadn't gotten into the wrong field, since the field did not have a soul, or at least the literature did not express the knowing of a soul.

At this time, I decided to do a literature review via the oral tradition. I was able to locate some wise elders who were able to describe the soul-wounding process. They explained that the ancestral wounding that occurred in the community was being passed down through the generations. They gave accounts of how the genocide had occurred in their area. Between the years 1870 and 1900, at least 80% of the population had been systematically exterminated. In addition, they explained how the earth had been wounded and how, when the earth is wounded, the people who are caretakers of the earth also are wounded at a very deep soul level. Earth wounding speaks to the process whereby people become destructive to the natural environment and disturb the natural order. My thinking was deeply affected by the schism in my psyche between the Western system I was studying and the life-world presented within this oral tradition.

Almost immediately, it became apparent that the results of the needs assessment went against all of the collective wisdom and research of the mental health profession. Results expected of such an assessment would include issues such as high alcoholism rates, high suicide rates, family dysfunction, and hopelessness. Actual data revealed a concept that was foreign to me as a professional because that concept did not exist in the literature of that time—namely, the problem was perceived by the community as the "soul wound."

At this time, I found some of the research literature emerging from Israeli studies on intergenerational post traumatic stress (Shoshan, 1989; Solomon, Kotter, & Mikulincer, 1988). This concept later became known as intergenerational trauma, historical trauma, and the Native American concept of soul wound. These concepts all present the idea that when trauma is not dealt with in previous generations, it has to be dealt with in subsequent generations. Initial research by the abovementioned Israeli studies indicated that not only is the trauma passed on intergenerationally, but it is cumulative. Therefore, there is a process whereby unresolved trauma becomes more severe each time it is passed on to a subsequent generation.

Intergenerational trauma is a concept, clinical issue, and fact that has been widely explored in recent literature (Brave Heart, 1999; Brave Heart-Yellowhorse, 2000, 2003; Danieli, 1998; Duran & Duran, 1995; Duran, Duran, Yellowhorse & Yellowhorse, 1998; Epstein, 1979). Although it is a relatively new idea in Indian country, the concept of intergenerational trauma and the effects on present-day Aboriginal people are receiving greater attention by academics, health providers, and community members. Treatment programs are modifying clinical strategies, and funding sources are beginning to require knowledge of historical trauma in order for funding to be awarded. This new approach to some of the problems facing Aboriginal communities includes a fundamental paradigm shift.

An understanding of historical context must underlie the use of intervention strategies with Native People (Manson, 2004). Until recently, the concept of historical trauma has been known only as theory in Western systems, although historical trauma has been readily accepted as a reality of daily existence in Native communities. Preliminary empirical study regarding historical trauma in Indian country reveals results that have serious implications for present-day Native Americans, therapists, and healers. The empirical data provide further support for the development of new methods that will lead to a new way of addressing the issues facing Original People. Research examining historical trauma indicates:

- "Remarkable prevalence among the contemporary parent generation" of measured historical trauma.
- "Thoughts about historical losses appear to be associated with symptoms of emotional distress." Symptomatic manifestations of the perception of historical loss include anger, anxiety, and depression.
- "The 'holocaust' is not over for many American Indian people. It continues to affect their perceptions on a daily basis and impinges on their psychological and physical health." (Whitbeck, Adams, Hoyt, & Xiaojin, 2004, pp. 127–128)

Internalized Oppression: Bitten by the Vampire

Paradigm shifting is not an easy task, and the effort usually creates awareness that other areas of the paradigm are being influenced by the new way of thinking. One impact of the awareness of historical trauma is the notion of internalized oppression, or as it was known previously, identification with the aggressor (Freud, 1967). Identification with the aggressor is a phenomenon observed in clinical settings in which the patient presents with physical, psychological, epistemic, and cultural violence, and the victim identifies with the perpetrator in a variety of ways.

Michael Butz (1993) presents an interesting clinical study in which internalized oppression is understood through the mythology of the vampire. Early on, Butz discovered that the patient, who was a victim of physical violence, did not want to communicate verbally. (The violence in these cases may be physical, sexual, spiritual, or emotional. It is important that the energy of violence receive the attention. The spirit of violence manifests in different symptoms, but the interventions are targeted at the cause, not merely at the symptoms.) Butz decided to go along with this and made nonverbal materials, including art supplies, available in the session. During the next session, the young boy drew a picture of a vampire. When Butz brought the picture to the case conference, it was not clear what the vampire image represented. A clinical decision was made to wait for more projective material to emerge in order to help amplify or interpret the image—to gain insight into what the psyche was trying to convey. At the next case conference, Butz presented additional projective material from the patient, who had created another vampire drawing, an indication that the image did not yet have an interpretation. The patient drew similar images a couple more times. At this point, Butz began researching vampires. Thematic study of vampire literature gave him the insight to amplify the patient's projective drawings of vampires.

Emerging themes revealed several traits of vampires. Vampires have a tendency to work at night and in darkness; they are part of a secret society; they can be eradicated only by special spiritual means. Further, when they bite a victim, the victim becomes infected and also will become a vampire. These insights assisted in understanding that the patient's psyche was calling for very specific help. One kind of help the patient wanted was treatment that would protect him from becoming a vampire himself (Butz, 1993).

Insights that automatically arise from the vampire image provided some of the material needed to address the immediacy of the clinical situation. Although the usual treatment methods were being used, Butz realized that a deeper therapeutic approach was needed to address the vampire image and the implications that this brought to the clinical situation. Butz engaged the patient in treatment that encompassed addressing spiritual issues within the family in addition to ongoing systemic family therapy, supportive therapy, and insight-oriented treatment.

Through a shifting in treatment paradigms, the patient is allowed to validate an injury that occurred at different levels. Injuries of this type occur at the physical, psychological, and spiritual aspects of the person. Patients quickly understand that the body can heal in a reasonable time, and psychological interventions can bring understanding and insight into the situation. Still, symptoms persist after psychological and medical treatment occurs. Once the notion of spiritual injury is introduced, patients usually shift their perspective and begin to search for deeper healing of the spirit. Butz's case example illustrates how the patient sought treatment to rid himself of the infection that the vampire injected into his soul. In essence, some of the vampire or perpetrator is already in the person after the person has been victimized.

It is important to note that the case above involved violence of a sexual nature. Regardless of the type of violence inflicted on the victim, there are similar psychological and spiritual aspects of the case that must be attended to. It is true that sexual violence has a deeper impact on the spirit and has to be dealt with in a delicate manner, as will be illustrated in the case study in Chapter 6. Other types of violence also have some of the spiritual implications found in sexual violence, as is the case in domestic violence between adults and violence toward children.

"Psychology" and "Soul Study"

I realize that the use of the terms *spirit* and *soul* may have some readers feeling uneasy because these terms are not part of the Western psychological terminology. However, the literal definition of our profession has deep roots that are enmeshed with spiritual metaphor. It is important to be cognizant that the word *psychology* literally translates into "study of soul." When asked, many of our fellow professionals identify themselves as "psychotherapists." Again, through a simple etymological regression, we find that this identity literally translates into "soul healer." The task that our profession pursues via soul healing is eradication of "psychopathology," which translates into "soul suffering."

Most of the root metaphors required for the task at hand have existed in the psychological profession for millennia. A simple linear approach to this would yield the question, "What happened to cause us to lose the essential meaning of our root metaphor?" Through the process of the so-called enlightenment and the Cartesian splitting of the world, we literally have done just that. We have been split off from our world-soul. It follows that if the healer is split from her soul, she will not be able to facilitate the integration of soul in her patients. Is it possible that our profession also has been infected by the vampire's bite imposed by the Cartesian objectification of the life-world? Objectification of the life-world into a subject–object relationship helps us to rationalize away the reality of the soul.

Western-trained therapists are trained to think within a prescribed paradigm that targets pathology. If this strategy does not work, then the patient may be further diagnosed with personality or characterological disorders, which, in the worldview of the *Diagnostic and Statistical Manual* used to diagnose mental disorders (American Psychiatric Association, 2000), are very difficult to treat. At this point, the patient may be left feeling frustrated and in many cases may choose to self-medicate with alcohol or illicit substances.

Cognitive therapies are the flavor of the decade at this point in time. From a philosophical standpoint, it is interesting that therapy focuses on cognition when the root of the word *psychology* is soul. Between the root of the word *psychology* and the world of clinical practice there appears to be an inconsistency at best and, perhaps, dishonesty at worst. Most Native People believe that they are more than just the cognitions that flow endlessly through the realm of awareness, and it is in these "other" aspects of the personality where there may be a place in which therapy/healing needs to happen. If we inflict a system that is based only on cognitions, as in the logocentric Euro-American tradition, we are committing hegemony (imposing a different worldview on someone) on the patient who believes otherwise. This type of cultural incompetence illustrates how someone operating from innocent ignorance actually can practice a form of hegemony that goes against all of the principles of our profession.

THE PSYCHOLOGY OF THE HEALER

The purpose of this book is to discuss clinical strategies that emerge out of a psychology of historical trauma, while maintaining the principles of cultural competence. I present archetypal material in its most root metaphoric fashion in order to sidestep some of the ego's defense mechanisms that are ready to diffuse spiritual phenomena via logical positivistic machinations of the mind. In order to discuss these issues, it is imperative also to delve into the psychology of the healer. Usually, discussions focus on the pathology or suffering of the patient, under the pretense that the patient's suffering exists in a vacuum. This type of psychologizing perpetrates blaming-the-victim approaches. When therapists engage in blaming-the-victim, we are participating in a process that has close association to some of the dynamics mentioned above, including projections of our own repressed shadow—in other words, our blind spots get in the way of the therapeutic process.

In essence, we have all internalized much of the personal and collective wounding of our culture. Our culture has been affected by a long history of violence against other cultures, which continues to the present. The wounding that is sustained by the collective culture has an impact on the psyches of the individuals in the society. The fact that the soul has been eradicated from our healing circle is indicative of a collective wounding process that has never been grieved or healed. It is from this wounded inner self that we, in the mental health field, seek to wound others, through the secrecy and darkness of our practice, and we attempt to ward off our shadow through exhaustive ethical codes. Ethical codes cannot make a soul healer out of anyone. These codes are usually there to avoid the most obvious perpetrators; well-defended ones can continue on their iatrogenic practice well "under the radar" of the code of ethics.

THE RAPE OF TURTLE ISLAND

At this time the reader may recall the idea of the vampire metaphor discussed earlier. This metaphor can be used to describe some of the problems inherited by the Native People of "Turtle Island," as the Western hemisphere is known in Native cosmology. The colonial process experienced by these people can be described as a collective raping process of the psyche/soul of both the land and the people. It is the inclusive life-world that becomes the victim of such an assault. As mentioned before, abuse occurs at the physical, psychological, and spiritual levels. Therefore, the issue must be addressed at all of these levels. Healing of the body, mind, and spirit is further compounded by the fact that the trauma occurs at the personal, community, and collective levels.

Issues regarding clinical practice within a culturally competent model become more complex when we consider the psychology of identification with the aggressor and of internalized violence and oppression. At this point, we have a clinical picture that must be assessed and treated from all of these points of reference: Western clinical practice, internalized oppression, historical trauma, and Traditional Aboriginal theory. A task of this nature is a Herculean one at best (requiring great strength) and Sisyphean at worst (as frustrating as the task of rolling a stone up a hill only to have it roll back), and it's little wonder that ongoing systems of care have such difficulty with patients presenting with intergenerational trauma and internalized oppression.

It would be an understatement to assert that providers must be aware of cultural competence and methods of treatment in order to understand the clinical ideology I am describing. Frustrations incurred by providers who are not prepared to deal with these issues may be manifested through a dynamic of blaming-the-victim. Patients will be further traumatized. Needless to say, this becomes the dynamic that allows further vampire projections to occur, and the patient may worsen and/or drop out of treatment.

Internalized Oppression as a Collective Ailment

The death of Crazy Horse is a well-known part of history within Indian country and not so well known in other segments of our society because much of the history of Original People is excluded in most American classrooms. Therefore, I will recount the manner in which Crazy Horse died. Crazy Horse was being led to a specific house on the Fort Robinson Army camp. Right before he entered the little house, he was detained by some of the Native People present. One of the Native men came behind Crazy Horse and stabbed him in the back with a bayonet (Marshall, 2004).

The death and vision of Crazy Horse regarding his death give us a clear understanding that he already understood the process of how violence can be internalized by a group of people.

Crazy Horse had a dream early on in his life in which he clearly saw the dynamics of internalized oppression symbolized in the manner in which he died at the hands of his own relatives.

> A lightning mark was painted across one side of his face. On his bare chest were blue hailstones. Behind them to the west as they galloped was a dark, rolling cloud rising higher and higher. From it came the deep rumble of thunder and flashes of lightning. The horse was strong and swift and it changed colors: red, yellow, black, white and blue. Bullets and arrows suddenly filled the air, flying at the horse and the rider, but they all passed without touching them. Close above them flew a red-tailed hawk, sending its shrill cry. People, his own kind suddenly rose up all around and grabbed the rider, pulling him down from behind. (Marshall, 2004, p. 72)

Once an individual or a collective society receives a soul wound of the magnitude that was perpetrated on Turtle Island, severe consequences manifest through the victims themselves. It is a historical fact that genocide has been perpetrated on the inhabitants of Turtle Island. Native Peoples suffered a holocaust of incredible magnitude, which can be understood clearly when history shows us how the population decreased as part of the holocaust perpetrated (Churchill, 1998; Thornton, 1987).

Atrocities committed by the onrush of colonial mania are part of the hidden transcripts of American history. Such atrocities must be mentioned in order to honor those who gave their lives. They include Sand Creek massacre, Wounded Knee massacre, the Long Walk of the Navajo, the Trail of Tears, the Long Walk of the Maidu People, and the burning of hundreds of Original People at James Town, which later became the celebration of Thanksgiving in our society. There are many other instances of genocide that contributed to the soul wound of the Original Peoples of Turtle Island. Our mythological, physical, and spiritual life-world was raped by an undifferentiated masculine mythology. In essence, the vampire bit the life-world known as Turtle Island, and the infection of the poison injected by the vampire has not been eradicated.

Why should this be of concern? Why even bring it up? I believe that this is one of the most important hurdles for Aboriginal People to overcome. Manifestation of the internalized soul wound is found in many facets of life, such as domestic violence, suicide, family dysfunction, community dysfunction and violence, institutional violence and dysfunction, tribal/ political infighting and violence, spiritual abuse and violence, and epistemic violence. I realize that these are sensitive areas that have remained as the last sacred cows in our communities, but the time has arrived to face the reality of history and of the present moment. These diagnoses are not made without a context or point of reference. I have been working with communities, individuals, and institutions in Indian country for over 2 decades. During this time, clinical and ethnographic reports have led to the formulation of these diagnostic areas of concern.

Although there are diverse manifestations of internalized oppression, there is a common thread that weaves all of them together. The pain and learned helplessness of internalized oppression continue to plague our relatives despite massive amounts of interventions that have been provided to treat the symptoms of individuals. Eventually, what is needed is a preventive intervention that addresses these issues at the source. Initially, what is required is awareness of the problem. Interventions then can be developed.

Internalized oppression is a wound that, like the vampire bite, becomes embedded as the individual or group is undergoing the abuse or trauma. Unless the victim is able to consciously explore the dynamics of the abuse and find meaning in the situation, that individual is doomed to repeat the abuse on someone or something else. Clear and insightful examples of this are given in the extraordinary insight provided by Victor Frankl (1959). Frankl relates how one of his fellow Holocaust survivors could not wait to get blood on his hands as he entertained fantasies of revenge. It is interesting that this survivor was expressing these fantasies just hours after liberation. One can see that the survivor had been bitten by the vampire of aggression. He was already infected with the same anger and vengeance as was carried by those who had committed atrocities against him and his fellow human beings.

Domestic Violence

Inflicting pain on loved ones is one of the most obvious manifestations of the internalized vampire's infection that pervades our communities. This type of violence can be understood as the projection of the internalized oppressor onto a related person. Internalized self-hate finds an object upon which to cathect (cleanse) or release the internalized pain. The individual directs the narcissistic injury onto someone who can represent him. The victim then carries the injury for him. Violence toward individuals close to the injured person thus results in some immediate relief, followed by remorse and another dose of internalized shame and guilt. According to Curry (1972),

> The explicit and conscious act of killing involves the affirmation of life, which is nourished by that which is killed. . . . Death belongs to life, perhaps not as specifically as the phrase "destructive love" suggests. But they are nevertheless related. The patient has not actually committed murder; he is, we may quickly conclude, only killing an image of himself. (p. 103)

If we juxtapose the psychological picture painted by Curry on the internalized oppression caused by historical trauma, we can begin to understand why the level of violence is so high in our communities.

Cycles of internalized shame and pain are only too well known, and our clinics abound with families forced into treatment or seeking treatment as a last resort. Unfortunately, some recent violence treatment models are pathologizing and result in additional guilt that the perpetrator is expected to absorb. Of course, having the perpetrator absorb more guilt and shame will only ensure that there is more shame to cathect (cleanse) at a later time. Thus, the treatment intended to heal actually contributes to further violence. Most treatment approaches do not remotely reflect the ideas in this book. Treatment efforts are directed toward ameliorating the symptoms of the victims. The so-called perpetrator usually is left to legal interventions: attempts to control the social world of the perpetrator, including incarceration, so that the opportunities for acting out are minimized. Interventions such as behavioral and psychodynamic strategies serve as a pretense to healing the perpetrator who is suffering from an internalized soul wound and the causes of the soul wound. The perpetrator is left feeling as if he is a "defective Indian," with little hope of choosing his identity from a wider spectrum of narratives.

If instead such violence is understood within an accurate historical context, the family will be able to step into a more objective treatment paradigm (such as the treatment approaches discussed later in this book). Instead of feeling like a dysfunctional and defective system, the family will be able to understand the choices allowed it by history that brought it to the point of having defective behaviors. These behaviors can be rewritten into the family's "new" story, which then can have a new ending. This is not to excuse the family from present responsibility for its own history. Instead, the family will be able to empower itself through the creation of a new myth for the family system that will include the overcoming of overwhelming historical intrusions. In effect, the family can feel powerful because it has been able to endure and to heal from the brutal history of its family, clan, and tribe. The narrative then shifts from a pathological one to one in which the family is healing. Further, the family is providing the historical context for subsequent generations to reinvent themselves as necessary to continue life in a more balanced life-world.

Institutional Violence

Institutional violence is part of a similar dynamic. Wherever I travel in Indian country, I encounter narratives about how some agency or institution has been the tool of violence for someone within that community. Many of our institutional leaders are themselves inheritors of the soul-wounding process. Within the past 25 years, the sobriety movement has focused on healthier communities and has helped many of our community and agency leaders to attain sobriety. Unfortunately, many leaders have attained sobriety without insight regarding the soul-wounding process that led them to use alcohol to help them anesthetize their pain.

Internalized pain continues to manifest itself through the same process described earlier. Trauma and soul wounding internalized personally or collectively through the inheritance of historical trauma continue to haunt some of the people leading our communities. Internalized oppression by some leaders is expressed in community and work environments in which administrative subordinates or community members are systematically abused. Violence manifested in an administrative or bureaucratic setting can be described as colonial bureaucratic violence. This type of violence, perpetrated by the people who are supposed to be caretakers of the community, is a violation that further alienates people from the collective family and isolates them in the society where they can be victimized by the oppressive forces in the culture.

A few years ago, I was invited to provide training in historical trauma for a band of tribes. While I was waiting to go up to the podium to present, an elderly woman approached me. After we greeted each other, she pointed to the podium where many officials were sitting. She said, "That is where most of the problem in our community is." The elderly woman was talking about institutional oppression, violence, and bureaucratic inertia represented by her community leaders. She observed that the leaders in her community had forgotten their charge of caring for the people. Instead, she observed that the leaders had become selfish and were working for themselves. Selfishness was evidenced by policy implementation in which leaders' family members gained financially from policy decisions. This is not to say this is the case in every community, but it does occur in some instances.

Pain is inflicted not only by leaders within Native communities but also through a more subtle institutionalization of dysfunction in our mental health institutions. Dysfunction in healing institutions is perpetuated by hiring and retaining staff who are not culturally competent and through the implementation of strictly Western medical models of treatment, which maintain the process of colonization. By operating health institutions in this manner, we ensure that people seeking help will continue to suffer from the illnesses that brought them there in the first place.

The power held by these colonized mental health administrators and tribal leaders of Indian country takes on a shadow (negative) quality if the administrator or leader has not become aware and healed from his personal and collective soul wound. One method by which these "mini-emperors" retain power is through support systems within the bureaucracy whose sole purpose is to maintain the power structure. Another method is the hiring and retaining of incompetent administrators and providers who will not question the power base of the system.

Data indicating a lack of community improvement, regardless of the amount of programmatic resources, attest to the fact that these programs have done little to ameliorate social problems in the community. Instead, many programs merely have become employment opportunities for those who agree with the ongoing colonial process. Due to this type of institutional and systemic violence, many gifted Native people prefer not to work within their communities and find work elsewhere. This leads to a "brain drain" in the community and maintains a dysfunctional and ineffective system.

In my work experience, I have observed many examples of institutional violence in our communities. There are many instances in which Native leaders prefer to have non-Native People working for them because they have internalized the belief that Native People are not as competent or capable. Abuse of Native staff by White supervisors is condoned in many settings because it is believed that the supervisors must be right. This belief in White authority is a legacy inherited from the boarding school era. One of the most widespread examples of institutional violence rooted in internalized oppression is the mistreatment of Traditional Healers by clinical personnel across Indian country.

The extent of colonization in our institutions has allowed hegemony, epistemic violence, and oppression of cultural norms to flourish. Agencies and institutions prefer models of service delivery that are entrenched in Western ideology, and Aboriginal models often are regarded as subservient and invalid. In the past, funding mechanisms encouraged these behaviors, but that is not as widespread now due to the cultural competency requirements of many funding sources. Currently, many of our institutions and agencies have been colonized into a psychology of "lactification" as defined by Franz Fannon (1963). This psychology lends itself to placing a higher value on European and Western values than on Original Peoples' epistemology.

STARTING A NEW NARRATIVE

At this point, there are few good answers to these forms of violence. Theories abound in the mental health field, and answers are sought in the judicial system. Although much effort has gone into searching for explanations and answers, the problems remain in the families and communities, with little hope for long-term healthy resolution. My method of searching for answers to this issue is very simple and begins by posing a simple question: "Where did you learn how to do this?"

This simple question allows the person to begin the archeology of the psyche that eventually will lead to an understanding of the soul wound or historical trauma. In my clinical work, such simple questions are crucial to bring clarity to the patient's situation. Once the questions are posed, patients make the necessary historical regressions to find the time and place where the behavior was learned. The patient finds where the vampire infected her family system. This approach allows the patient to depathologize and thus liberate herself while retaining responsibility for her behavior. Patients are greatly relieved to find out that they are not defective human beings. Instead, they are reacting to the context of history that systematically has inflicted these soul wounds.

To this most basic question, the usual answer is, "From my family or my parents." A logical follow-up question is, "Where did they learn this from?" This follow-up question allows the patient to begin to objectively observe the historical process in which certain behaviors have been instilled, and other behaviors systematically have been eradicated, within the family system. Behaviors that were eradicated through the colonization process were those involving Native ways of being in the life-world. Eradication of the Native life-world was attempted through a long process of genocide, ethnocide, and cultural hegemony. Asking these simple questions allows the patient and community to embark on the process of formulating a counter-hegemonic narrative to replace the colonial oppressing ideology.

A new narrative serves as a beginning. I must emphasize that the treatment process must include proven Western methods as well as the ideas discussed in this book. It would be naive to believe that simply making someone aware of the soul-wounding process would provide a magical solution. Excellent clinical interventions must be part of the overall strategy. I merely am focusing on the methods that are not known by our present treatment method.

The new narrative can begin to emerge only after the historical issues have been addressed. This is a difficult area, especially for non-Native providers, partly because non-Native providers usually begin to internalize guilt, which generates defensive reactions. These defense reactions become problematic in the therapeutic process because they take on a countertransference quality, thus awakening unresolved collective issues for the provider. If the therapist does not become aware of these reactions, they may take on a shadow quality and become destructive to the patient.

This is not to say that treatment and a new narrative cannot occur with non-Native providers. However, the non-Native providers also must be able to make a serious analysis of their own history and take responsibility for that history. In this manner, the providers are involved in a narrative therapy of their own, and in this honest historical vessel the wounding itself can be healed. Parallel narratives can emerge that will be liberating to both patient and healer, thus facilitating a more collective healing of the soul wound.

If the provider is Native, there are also precautions that must be taken. To assume that one understands the issues merely by virtue of belonging to the group, can be a trap. Native therapists must be careful that their own shadow projections are not activated in the countertransference process. For example, the Native therapist may respond to the history with anger that merges with the patient's anger, thus worsening the problems while validating them because the therapist is in a position of power. Therapists must be cognizant of the history and their own blind spots, as in any other treatment paradigm.

Therefore, it is critical that appropriate supervision and consultation be available to therapists working with Original People. Asking simple questions rooted in a historical context is one method that at least allows us to see the vampire as it lurks in the recesses of the psyche's shadow. Once awareness is focused on the vampire, change will occur. Interventions can be made before the vampire reacts. A community story can emerge from these efforts that will honor the effects of the historical context that previously was ignored. From this new story, individuals, families, and communities can move toward a collective healing that will have an impact on the overall society.

CHAPTER 2

Over Pathologizing
Original People

> One group of people walk toward the fire, into the fire, and the
> other toward the cool flowing waters. No one knows which is
> blessed and which is not.
> —Jelaladdin Rumi, 12th-century Sufi mystic (Barks, 1977)

IN MY WORK with Original People and the systems that serve Original People, I have become aware of some of the particular ways in which many health and mental health providers deal with patients from these communities. Many of the healers' behaviors are embedded in their own history. Some healers and therapists also are living and working with their own intergenerational trauma, which remains unsolved in many instances. When therapists and healers do not deal with their own history, they bring unconscious contents into the therapeutic setting. The natural consequence of this is projection of unconscious fantasies and ideas onto the patient. This projective process is known as transference.

Transference is a phenomenon that has received much attention in Western psychology (Freud, 1913; Jung, 1954). The transference process can be described as projection of unresolved unconscious contents onto an object or person who may possess similarity in character or in physical nature. A basic image of transference was given by Jung (1954) when he said that in order for transference to occur, there must be a hook for one to hang one's coat on. The idea of having a hook makes sense when considering physical appearance, but is not as easily observable when the projected contents are of a purely psychological nature.

In the Traditional Native world, transference can be understood as Freud and Jung understood it. In addition, transference in the Native world can encompass a spiritual aspect that is interpreted literally. That is, energy actually is transferred from one being to another. For example, Clements (1932) describes the sorcerer's projection and the illness that can

29

result from such projection. In addition to the possibility of making someone sick by projecting illness, there is the possibility of helping someone get well by projecting good healing energy.

TRANSFERENCE TOWARD ORIGINAL PEOPLE

Our modern society continues to provide instances of negative projections toward Native People. Film and other media persist in negative representation of the Native life-world in modern society. Identity of Native People is affected at a deep emotional level by the images portrayed in films, television, and other literature. Native people continue to be described as if they were living in the distant past and are assigned negative stereotypical portrayals. One identity is the portrayal of the Native person as a drunkard who is lazy, impulsive, and shiftless.

Equally important is the projection of spiritual nobility or of being knowledgeable of spiritual mysteries not known to other people. In this projection, Native People are seen as having special spiritual qualities that make them more in tune with natural processes. In addition, Native People are perceived as having special healing qualities. These projected fantasies can have widespread detrimental effects on the life of the individual and community because the projected fantasies of some non-Native People are supported in the popular media and are accessible to all Native People living in the modern world.

Projection of these fantasies may be detrimental psychologically because they may cause identity confusion. If people are not able to live up to the identity that has been projected on them, this may cause alienation and in more serious instances may be the underlying cause of emotional or psychological splitting. Also, the inability to live up to projected fantasies may cause people to regress to a safer psychological state, which may help them live up to the fantasy in their own individual life-world. As a result of struggling to reach a nonexistent ideal, the individual may begin to feel an emptiness that can be manifested as a loss of self, or depersonalization. On one hand, we have the fantasy of the ideal image, and on the other there is reality, and it becomes increasingly difficult to harmonize ideal and real as a single personality. The splitting process that may occur can lead to other emotional problems, as well as substance abuse and alcoholism, which arise as an attempt to deal with the turmoil caused by this identity confusion.

The importance of this type of transference to the present-day Native seeking therapy is that these fantasies and projections are part of the psychological makeup of many therapists. I do not intend to blame the victim in this case. Even though some of our training may involve brief discussion of transference, there is little mention or training that deals with therapists projecting fantasies of the noble savage or a negative stereotype on the person seeking help.

DIAGNOSIS AS A NAMING CEREMONY

Projection of fantasies can arise during the assessment and diagnostic processes that may be understood as a naming ceremony. Naming ceremonies are part of Native traditions and are used to assign spiritual identities to those receiving a name. Therefore, the naming ceremony performed by a healer or therapist has deep implications to the individual and community. In essence, assigning stereotypical diagnoses to Native People as a group has been problematic because none of the diagnoses assigned to Native People consider the historical factors that are of critical importance in this process. (I have not been able to find any acknowledgment of historical trauma in the DSM-IV and therefore feel safe in making the assumption that diagnosing Native People is not an accurate process.)

The patient goes through a diagnostic process that she perceives as a naming ceremony that literally gives her an identity of pathology. However, this identity is often an unconscious pathology being projected by the therapist. The patient then takes on the identity of being sick and in so doing carries the illness being projected by the therapist into her psychological makeup. Iatrogenic illness of this sort can be healed only when the therapist withdraws the projection, or conscious awareness is given to the patient by someone else, allowing the patient to let go of the projection. In my experience, therapists rarely take back projections and the second type of intervention is needed.

Over the years, I have had many patients who identify themselves as a diagnosis and not by their given name. Many of these patients are quick to tell their new therapist that they are depressed, anxious, alcoholic, and so on. Their identity has been crystallized through the unconscious naming ceremony of the diagnostic process. Within some of the belief systems of Aboriginal People, there is the notion that once a name is given, it remains until a more powerful ceremony occurs. Therefore, one of the first tasks for the therapist working in Indian country is decolonizing the individual from the ideology of diagnosis and naming.

The fact that diagnosis is such a pathologizing and colonizing activity does not mean that diagnosis is a totally useless activity. If the healer/ therapist is able to make the diagnosis within a proper cultural context, then this is part of the therapeutic/healing encounter. As part of their healing work, Traditional Healers take part in diagnosing patients as part of the treatment encounter. The mind-set and psychology that the Traditional Healer utilizes as part of the naming of the illness in order to extract or balance the energy creating the problem for the patient is very different from the Western medical model approach.

Traditional Healing in most Aboriginal cultures is based on the belief that illness itself has a consciousness that relates to the psyche and/or body of the individual. Belief that illness is conscious leads to the idea that all illness has a distinct purpose that eventually will teach and bring wholeness to the individual. It is worthwhile to reiterate Clements's (1932) classical analysis of sickness and healing, which delineates five core concepts of healing and illness. Clements asserts that sickness may be caused by object intrusion, sorcery, breech of taboo, spirit possession, or loss of soul. It is clear from this formulation that illness of any type, when seen from the perspective of the psychology of Native People, is quite different from that viewed from the perspective of the Euro-American individual.

The key purpose in naming a sickness in Traditional Healing is to restore a relationship with the energy of the sickness. Instead of the fearful antagonistic purpose of diagnosis in Western healing, the illness energy is not perceived as inherently evil nor is it something to be extinguished. Once the patient and healer discover the identity of the illness, the illness can be asked about its purpose and about what it is trying to teach the patient and the healer. The relationship with the illness affects the psyche of the healer and thus the healer also must have a relationship with the illness. Otherwise, the healer may contract the illness in the same way therapists contract burnout.

Illness is viewed as having a dualistic nature. If the energy of the illness is not harmonized, then the illness will have a negative impact on the patient. Harmonizing with an illness occurs by making conscious contact with the consciousness of the illness (this will be dealt with in depth in Chapter 6). It is important to note that harmonizing with the illness is not related to the Western notion of prognosis. The patient may die from the illness even after a harmonious relationship has been established, because the lesson of the illness may be to assist the patient into the next realm, known as death. Therefore, the root metaphor in Traditional Healing is that of relationship versus a metaphor of pathologizing, as is found in Western approaches.

In my clinical work in Indian country, most of the patients presenting themselves for help have perceived their illness as an entity possessing their consciousness. Many times, patients have described the etiology of their illness as the result of someone "witching" them. When this "witching" process is discussed in a respectful manner that validates the patient's worldview, the patient is able to gain insight regarding the problem. In addition, the patient then is able to address the specific consciousness or complex causing the problem.

Many Native People are diagnosed with a variety of psychological problems, but the underlying causes of the diagnoses usually are left undiagnosed and untreated. This is a great disservice to Native People who approach therapists or healers for help with their life problems, many of which are deeply rooted in a historical context. In addition, the diagnosis of a whole group may be seen within the Native life-world as a collective naming ceremony that gives a negative identity to Native people as a whole.

In present-day settings, it is well known that poor people receive the poorest quality of health and mental health care. Because of disparity between medical and psychological insurance coverage, many in our society do not receive adequate care for their emotional and psychological problems. Given the low socioeconomic status of most Native People, it is a logical step to infer that Native People are subject to less than adequate health care. Also, because of the lack of opportunity afforded Native People, mental health providers are for the most part a product of the collective culture in which they have been reared. Even the most caring people have difficulty surviving the socialization process of graduate programs that heavily promote Western medical models and treat other models of healing and therapy as subservient.

An understanding of historical context is essential in the effort to deconstruct what occurs in present-day clinical practice. When history, the theory of transference, and impacts of projection are juxtaposed, it becomes possible to infer what happens in modern-day therapeutic settings. It is not unusual for people in the therapy field to take issue with this type of historical analysis because most of our training to become clinicians does not include sociohistorical factors. We need only reflect on what transference actually is and this fear can be left behind. Transference projections, according to the classical definitions, are based on prior history (Freud, 1913). The simplest form of transference occurs when the patient's history with his mother or father is projected onto the therapist. Countertransference then would involve the history of the therapist toward significant people in his life who remind him of the patient. Therefore, personal and collective historical experience is the sine qua non of the whole transference phenomenon as it manifests in the healing setting.

THERAPISTS AS PERPETRATORS OF HISTORICAL TRAUMA

After 2 decades of clinical and preventive work in Indian country, it has become apparent to me that there are dynamics between the clinician and the patient or community that can best be described through the application of transference theory. It is not my purpose to discuss classical transference theory because the idea of transference is over a century old and countless books and articles exist that deal with the topic in almost every imaginable scenario. One particular scenario that is not dealt with in most of the existing literature, however, is the projection of unconscious material onto a Native American patient by the therapist or healer.

Unconscious projections occur all the time in human interactions. It is of critical concern, however, when they occur in the healing or therapeutic setting, because these unconscious processes have a direct effect on the therapeutic relationship and outcome of treatment. It has become apparent to me that the dynamics of projections from the healer to the patient have additional fantasy material in the case of a Native American patient and a non-Native provider. These fantasies become more complex when juxtaposed with the dynamics of intergenerational trauma and the guilt this elicits from the healer (Duran & Duran, 1995). In order to have a critical understanding of these dynamics, it is necessary to deal with the historical context that influences these healing encounters. Therapists who do not understand this colonial diagnostic paradigm begin to project their helplessness onto the patient.

As far as I know, this will be the first time that the issue of historical transference of the perpetrator receives attention in our field. If there is such a construct as historical trauma, then there must be a parallel construct that also is passed on in some form to mental health professionals. This parallel process can be explained by the fact that most therapists in our society are from the so-called dominant culture. The term *dominant* signifies that they have dominated and continue to dominate someone. The ability to dominate is rooted in the perpetration of colonization and trauma on the Original People of Turtle Island. When the issue of responsibility is broached, clinicians may respond with guilt, and defensive mechanisms flourish. It is common to hear in our culture statements like, "I never owned slaves," or "I never killed any Indians. I am not a racist. Everyone has had their traumas. Why do we have to hear all this negativity?" And so on, ad nauseum.

Clinicians who are in positions of power can resort to more clandestine defensive maneuvers. We simply do not bring up these issues and if someone starts talking about them, we pathologize the patient, diagnose the patient with resistance, and wash our hands of the situation. When we do this, we leave our patients who are victims of historical trauma in an invalidated position, which can only serve to exacerbate their symptoms because now they are sure it must be they who are defective.

In order to stay true to historical context, clinicians must explore their own history and position of privilege. Many of our clinical brothers and sisters come from families that only two or three generations ago were directly involved in the so-called "manifest destiny" colonization process, which was instrumental in inflicting the soul wound. Now they are attempting to heal the third generation of Native People who received the soul wound from their very families. It might be helpful to imagine for a moment what is going on subconsciously and consciously in the mind of the patient who is still carrying the soul wound and all the symptoms that go with it. What if the clinician were to acknowledge his role in this soul-wounding process and began with an apology? I realize that this is clinical heresy and quickly the Freudian blank slate rule would become effective. Of course, healing then becomes hampered and ineffective.

CLINICAL RACISM IN INDIAN COUNTRY

In this section, I present a scenario that is typical in many treatment agencies throughout Indian country in the United States and Canada. In order to protect the confidentiality of the specific agencies and communities involved, the information is generalized so that no one group will feel unduly targeted. The situations depicted have been gathered through 2 decades of consulting with at least 50 agencies responsible for delivery of health, mental health, and alcohol treatment services. Some of the problems encountered and discussed here may seem to have a negative tone. It is difficult for me to be truthful and to appear positive when the lives of people are affected by the actions we take in clinical settings. It is in the spirit of bringing a more positive healing attitude to our field that I present the discussion that follows. I want to make sure that readers understand that it is possible to have a good and healthy clinical situation in a Native American setting if they are mindful of some of the issues presented.

First, I will discuss an issue that continues to emerge in both inpatient and outpatient settings where Native People are treated; I suspect other people of color have experienced similar situations. As a clinician and administrator, I have conducted programmatic reviews. The purpose of these reviews is to ensure that standards of practice are adhered to in both clinical and administrative procedures that are part of quality assurance designed to protect the public from possible harm. During these reviews, I have found some consistent issues that are very troubling, and I have coined the term "clinical racism" to describe some of these practices. These reviews have been conducted in settings staffed by licensed professionals who have been trained in the basics of delivering quality mental health services. At this point, cultural competency is not even part of the equation.

In some of the leading health care delivery agencies in Indian country, essential elements of basic clinical practice are usually lacking. Lack of proper charting procedures is very problematic and directly affects the quality of care that patients receive. It is remarkable that the above deficiencies exist, when one considers that most clinicians who work in Indian country also work in what are known as mainstream health settings. When confronted about the lack of minimum standards, the clinicians all acknowledge that they know how to deliver a minimum standard of care. Therefore, the simplest question is, "Why don't they do this in their work with Native People?" None of these clinicians would ever think about getting away with such inadequate clinical work in a "White" agency or hospital.

There is an attitude of not having to do as much for Native People who are considered to be "simplistic," as some clinicians have expressed to me. Because the fantasy of these clinicians is that Natives are not very sophisticated, it follows that the care they receive also can be unsophisticated and of lesser quality. Viewing people in a dehumanizing manner can only be described as racist, and because clinical practice is the issue, it makes sense to apply the term *clinical racism*.

Unfortunately, most of the providers who fall in the trap of "clinical racism" are in charge of programs, so their philosophy permeates the treatment system. At the lower echelons of the clinical ladder, we find Native individuals who are supervised by clinicians who see Natives in a negative light. This ideology is impressed on the Native clinicians, and they also begin to practice clinical racism because they are led to believe that this is sound clinical practice. After years of such practice, the system develops a bureaucratic inertia that is almost impossible to change without drastic action.

The administrative and clinical programs of agencies that serve Native clients usually are characterized by one of the following scenarios:

1. The director has an advanced degree and is not a Native American. Most directors profess to be culturally sensitive, but cultural sensitivity is not adequate. It is critical that all providers and administrators be culturally competent. Unfortunately, there are few established guidelines for cultural competence. Some of the cultural competence criteria that I would suggest include: knowing the history of the tribe, understanding the family system structure of the community, and practicing some of the basic competence issues brought up previously in the Introduction and Chapter 1 of this book. In clinics where there are some guidelines in place, they are not directly tied to performance evaluations, which renders the guidelines interesting but not very useful. When directors who are not Native American are hired, the countertransference issues mentioned previously are raised.

When the staff is non-Native and keeps up a pretense of cultural sensitivity, the reality that plays out in the treatment setting is one of therapist shadow projection. This well-known phenomenon usually is referred to in therapeutic circles as "blind spots." However, I do not believe that the problem is blindness, but the projection of shadow. Blindness implies that there is a true empty space, and this is not the case even with the most enlightened therapist. The shadow of the therapist crystallizes as pathology perceived in the patient.

2. The director is a Native who has been socialized into Western thinking. His clinical and administrative oversight are mostly from a Western point of view. If there are Native staff members who retain their cultural beliefs, this director will be a source of conflict. I have seen situations where Native directors actually oppress Native thought and validate the Western worldview in a manner that can only be described as internalized oppression. Patients will not benefit as much from the program because the staff will not be acting in a harmonious fashion. There are several programs to my knowledge that have deteriorated so badly that they closed.

In federally funded programs, hiring practices require adherence to "Indian preference," which gives a Native applicant the job if the individual is "minimally qualified." This is an interesting situation. Many Native applicants have undergone deep socialization into Western values in the process of getting an advanced degree. If these individuals, when hired, retain their socialization and adhere to Western methods, they may actually cause harm to the community since the community may feel betrayed by "one of their own."

Hiring practices will become increasingly interesting as more Natives go through graduate training. I have attended meetings that specialize in the recruitment and training of Native students. Many of the students do not identify with any aspect of Native culture and are basically Western in their cultural orientation and clinical practice. Therefore, just having a Native provider does not ensure cultural competence. We must strive to make cultural clinical competence a true competence that is an integral part of the students' training. In that manner, the true needs of communities will best be served.

3. The director is a Native person who maintains cultural beliefs and has great disdain for Western methods and thought. As with the reverse situation just described, this scenario also is doomed to fail especially if staff members are trained in Western methods. Lack of harmony will prevail, and appropriate treatment plans will not be possible. Many of the patients seen in these settings prefer and respond to Western methods. For instance, a family in need of behavior modification will do best with this method and may not necessarily need Traditional ceremony to remedy the problem. It is best to have flexibility in clinical and theoretical practice. Directors should encourage staff to be highly competent in their specialty area as well as being culturally competent. There should not be a competition to be "more Indian than thou," an aspect of internalized oppression that sets Native People against one another. Challenges to an individual's legitimacy as an Indian can be based on different attributes, such as being from a reservation, speaking the language, knowledge of ceremonies, skin tone, and so on. Such bickering will engender staff jealousies and conflicts that are not conducive to a healthy healing environment.

4. The director has integrated Western and Traditional Native clinical ideologies and administrative processes. This is the ideal situation. With this type of leadership, it is possible to have fluidity between the worldviews. The director is able to deal with staff and patients from both worldviews. It is easier to maintain harmony in this scenario than in any of the others because this is a true "postcolonial hybrid" situation. In addition, the director will be able to help train both Native and White students in a well-rounded and clinically competent manner that will best serve the community. After all, our work should be directed toward community wellness and not ego gratification.

In this chapter, I have explored the issue of transference in working with Native Americans. I believe that if some of the issues discussed are addressed by therapists, they will become more effective healers not just in the Native community but in general. I do not mean to imply that this is the last word in this area. Much more exploration is needed. In addition to clinical exploration, evaluation of the approach will be useful for making the methods more available to students and therapists at all levels of their training and professional life. It is my hope that an understanding of the implications of negative and positive transference on diagnosis and treatment will result in better patient care. Such insight also will enhance the practice of healers so that they find themselves part of a larger whole and their work has deep implications for healing society.

CHAPTER 3

The Healing/Therapeutic Circle

> This is the first account, the first narrative. There was nothing
> brought together, nothing which could make a noise, nor any-
> thing which might move, or tremble, or make noise in the sky.
> There was nothing standing; only the calm water, the placid sea,
> alone and tranquil. Nothing existed.
> —How the beginning of the universe is depicted by
> the Popol Vuh (Goetz & Morley, 1953, p. 81).

ALL THINGS as we know them have a beginning, middle, and ending. In the healing arena, we must be aware that the beginning,
middle, and ending have their own way of manifesting themselves. Things that are said at the different stages of the healing process
usually are dictated by a natural progression in the process. Interventions
and words that are perfectly acceptable toward the end of the healing process would be considered inappropriate in the beginning phases, before
an alliance has been formed. Of course, the beginning, middle, and ending could occur within a short span of time or the process may take longer. The therapist needs to be aware of the progression of healing at any
particular point in the relationship. This relationship involves the patient
as well as the pathological entities themselves (details of this will be discussed later).

During the past 2 decades, certain initial interventions have become
part of my therapeutic strategy for patient healing. Because I have been
in a supervisory capacity most of my career, I have encouraged the staff
that works with me to integrate some of these interventions into their own
clinical treatment methods. Initially, staff members who have been indoc-
trinated in academic Western therapeutic methods are resistant. Resistance
usually does not last because they see that some of the new approaches
actually work. The clinicians begin to work in an innovative mode that
brings a type of "Hawthorne effect" (the fact that something changes is
enough to create a change in the person's behavior even if the change is

one that the person should be familiar with) of newness and excitement to their clinical practice. In this chapter I will discuss some of the requirements of the actual setting as well as the inner setting of the healer in order to introduce the actual practice, which will follow.

IN THE VERY BEGINNING

As soon as a patient makes contact, I begin using liberation discourse so that the patient, even if she has never been in therapy, understands this will be a unique type of therapeutic experience. By liberation discourse, I mean that I do not use the language of authority and power that they have become accustomed to hearing in professional settings. Most people have a stereotype of the therapeutic process, and I want to move into a different modality right away. Because therapy has become popular, many patients have been in therapy or know something about what happens or is supposed to happen in therapy. I prefer to take a different approach. Many patients actually have a script of what therapy should be like, and I try to move beyond this perceived script as soon as possible.

I encourage all therapists to make the initial appointment themselves. In this manner, the patient can hear the actual therapeutic voice that will be part of his healing process. During this first conversation, it is important to ensure that the patient is not in imminent crisis and does not require some type of immediate medical attention. Once these issues are out of the way, it is time to start the acculturation assessment.

Acculturation assessment is done very informally. In actuality, this is not just an acculturation assessment; it is an assessment of how the patient relates to his particular tribal or pan-tribal Native life-world. Questions about tribal affiliation, ceremonial practice, the patient's understanding of his problem, and possible solutions are discussed in a short period of less than 5 minutes. Some of the questions are designed to gather information regarding the tribe, for instance, whether the patient is urban or reservation-based, and if Traditional Native practices are part of his life. Before the conversation is over and the appointment is made, I ask the patient to become aware of his dreams, to note them however he wants, and bring these to the first appointment. Sometimes, the patient will say that he does not dream. I simply let him know that it is alright not to dream, but that if he does, to bring the material to the session.

The manner in which I use dream material has some similarities to common Western methods used by our profession for some time. Some of the similarities have to do with the recording of the dream, understanding some wish fulfillment aspects of the dream, and exploring archetypal material in the dream and how this material may relate to the present situation. In addition, I use a spiritual framework of understanding dreams. I tell patients that at times, to understand the deeper issue causing them discomfort, we need to access their spirit for insight. In order to do this, we need to consult the dream process. Patients usually have an understanding that their dreams are important, but for the most part do not know how to relate to them.

I tell patients that the dream or dreamtime is a living entity and therefore requires that the patient display appropriate etiquette and manners. Patients are told that when they have a dream, they should acknowledge it with a gift. The gift offered to the dreamtime can be tobacco, food, water, cornmeal, or some other offering that they deem appropriate. This type of intervention is purely of Native origin. The distinctive type of relationship to the dreamtime calls for a different approach from others, such as the Freudian or Jungian methods (Freud, 1900/1980; Jung, 1977), in which dreams are treated as part of ego wish fulfillment or an aspect of complexes and archetypes. In Western approaches, dreams are within the personality, which makes it possible for an ego-centered personality to arise. In Traditional ways of understanding dreams, the personality is within the dream itself, which makes it difficult for the personality to become ego-oriented and easier to be part of the greater cosmology.

My reasoning for the initial dream intervention is so that the patient can realize fairly quickly that the intervention resides in her and that therapy facilitates the relationship to her inner process. This is important in the beginning as well as in termination of treatment. In addition, the patient, regardless of how acculturated she is, will be able to establish a relationship with dreams, which are very important to Traditional Native beliefs. Already, with the first phone call, the process of decolonizing has begun. Translated to the patient, this means that we are starting to talk using Indigenous metaphor, although we also can engage in colonial "White Man Talk" (as this is known in Indian country). As the therapy proceeds, we will be conscious at all times of what kind of "talk" we are engaging in.

Why is this even important? It is critical for Native patients to understand that part or all of their pathology or diagnosed pathology could have roots in the colonization process they have been involved in over several generations. Part of the treatment must include awareness of the emotional and/or psychological impact of this intergenerational oppression. By understanding the genesis of the problems, patients can assume responsibility for their lives and gain an objectivity that has not been available to them until this moment of awareness. For many patients it is the first realization that they are not "defective" or inferior human beings and that there are sociohistorical/political reasons for their problems.

It should be obvious that the issues brought up in Chapter 2 arise in this early phase of therapy. Patients expect to be pathologized based on many years of intergenerational medical model episodes. The first phase of therapy includes the naming ceremony or diagnosis that has been performed in their past experience in which they have been made to feel defective. Many Native People shy away from mental health systems unless they are in crisis, because they fear that being pathologized also will result in a loss of freedom—being either physically locked up or immobilized by medication. Therefore, a great stride has been taken in the initial stage by simply allowing the patient to get in touch with a part of life that is accessible to all human beings, that is, the dream, a critical part of the initial stage of treatment.

THE HEALING CONTAINER

Healing usually occurs in a container. Most Western practitioners talk about the boundaries of the therapeutic work. Therapeutic/healing boundaries usually are provided by an office or some other structure. When doing work of the type discussed in this book with Original People, it is imperative that the therapist/healer pay close attention to the container or the hermetic vessel, as it was called by our counterparts who practiced alchemy. The work requires an intuitive approach to the life-world, but intuition can be dangerous for both the patient and therapist if it is allowed to fly tangentially at will. Intuition must be balanced with knowledge and wisdom of the nature of illness and healing. Therefore, a metaphorical spiritual boundary must be put into place in order for the process to be contained and to allow patients space in which they can feel safe as their healing process emerges.

Having worked with Traditional Native healers for many years, I have noticed that they pay very close attention to the container and to ceremony. The notion that therapy is a ceremony is of critical importance. If it is not approached as a formal ceremony, most of what I will say in this book will be of little importance to the practitioner. Native Healers ensure that the ceremony is contained by either a physical or metaphorical structure. Even within a physical structure, the Native Healer will enact a metaphorical boundary in the form of smoke, offerings, encircling cornmeal around the patient, and so on.

I have been very conscious of providing a container, which is usually part of a larger container at a health agency or hospital. Rules that govern the physical environment in most of our Western settings require creativity in making an appropriate vessel or container for healing. Physical boundaries are easier to accomplish because these can take the form of objects, pictures, plants, and so on. Metaphorical healing boundaries can be more difficult because these may require the burning of certain plants, or tobacco, throwing cornmeal, and other appropriate offerings, depending on the tribe involved.

Over the years, I have accumulated several "power objects." These objects either are known to possess power derived through ceremony or are simply ones that Native culture has accepted as objects with healing power. A parallel can be found in Western traditions in the use of the Crucifix, Star of David, Caduceus, and so on. These objects should be visible to anyone who walks into the container or office. The Native patient will relate to these objects as much as she will relate to the therapist, either consciously or subconsciously.

In my therapeutic/healing container, I also have made a small burner out of clay in which I burn cedar, sage, or sweet-grass. These natural herbs have specific uses in ceremonial context and most Native People know that these are special to their life-world, even though many do not know their specific uses. It suffices that the patient knows that the healer/therapist is doing something special to prepare and purify the container for the therapeutic process. (As will be explained later, the smoke can be a form of therapeutic boundary between the healing container and some of the psychological/spiritual forces that are creating suffering in the life-world of the patient.) Most Native patients have an understanding of these smells and are grateful to be provided with a space that has been purified for the purpose of healing their wounded soul. Therefore, a lot of effort goes into the preparation of the vessel.

THE IDENTITY OF THE HEALER

The identity of the healer is also critical. Over the years, I have always asked interns and staff a simple question: "Who are you?" The question is not rhetorical, and the answer requires exploration into who they are as a person, who they are in the healing situation, and who they are in their life-world. Answers to the question of identity vary from their understanding of being an American, a clinician, an intern, a man or woman, and so on. Very few of the interns understand the question of identity as one relating to who they are as a spiritual being. The importance of spiritual identity starts to become clear as they begin to understand that a relationship with spiritual entities is part of the work that we do in the clinical world.

In most Traditional Healing cultures, the Healers embody the healing energy in their life and in all that they do. Western healers have a way of compartmentalizing their role as a healer from what they do in "real life." Therapists who want to work with Native Americans and include the ideas outlined in this work will have to decide whether to compartmentalize or to live life in accordance with healing traditions.

It is interesting and worth repeating that the literal translation of the word *psychotherapist* is "soul healer," yet few people in our field are aware of this, or even believe that there is such a thing as "soul." The life purpose of the "soul healer" is to help patients with their psychopathology, or soul suffering. Therefore, the definitions of healing in Western and Traditional cultures are consistent. All we need to do to achieve cultural competence is to engage with the healing tradition that is part of our genetic memory and be true to that tradition. It is the merging of these traditions that is the challenge for the modern Western-trained therapist who is working with Native Americans.

At this point, I ask the reader who is interested in the healing process, "Who are you?" If you are interested merely in techniques that will ameliorate behaviors in the short and even long term, then these ideas may not be for you. However, if you are even remotely interested in the notion of soul healing from the ongoing soul wounding that is encountered in every aspect of life in the modern corporate world, then I encourage you to read on. I realize that telling someone with an advanced degree that she shouldn't see a Native patient unless she is culturally competent may be difficult to accept.

Once you have decided that "soul work" is your cup of tea, that work becomes your first priority. Depending on your Traditional culture, this may take different forms, but the result is the same. Your own soul must be healed so that you can attend to the patient who is presenting with a wounded soul. You cannot do for others what you haven't done for yourself. It is imperative that you attend to your dreams and gain a deep understanding of the messages that your soul gives you through dreams, visions, and other synchronistic phenomena.

As a soul healer, you must re-evaluate your notions of sickness and healing. This is not to say that you have to throw out Western notions of healing. You must be open to other approaches to understanding how people's lives fall out of balance and must understand how the soul of the individual is influenced by some of the cosmological forces that affect the life-world, in both the personal and collective spheres.

Over the years that I was teaching courses in clinical practice, I would give students a year-long assignment to assist them with their identity. They would be asked to do a project in which they would find their tribe, the name of their tribal God, and their tribal creation story. Ninety-nine percent of these students were Euro-American or White folks. As part of the assignment, I would tell them that unless they were Jewish, the creation story in the Bible would not be acceptable because it was not their story.

As the reader can imagine, this assignment created quite a disturbance in the initial phase of the class and students thought that it made no sense. Of course, this was one of the purposes of the task—to remove them from their thinking function. In order for the therapist to make contact with a Native, or any other patient, the ancestors of the Healer must be known. The ancestors of the Healer and the ancestors of the patient also will be relating in the healing process. This was explained to the students, much to their despair.

When students complained of their inability to find their roots because they felt that they were "Heinz 57" or a mixture of cultures, I referred them to their dreams and asked them to be mindful of synchronistic events. By the second month or so, students were engaged in a process that had become quite interesting to them, both individually and collectively as a class. They began the process of identifying themselves as people standing in the center of the world and thus healing their own alienation. This understanding of being at the center provided the students with an identity that surpassed the identity that they previously had and allowed them to become acquainted with a way of relating to entities versus pathologizing patients. The rationale of this assignment lies in the question, "How can you guide someone who is alienated if you are alienated yourself?"

Another issue that I raised in this class was the notion of client-centered therapy. This idea does not make sense to many Original People. If the patient is centered, then he does not need to be seen for treatment. Instead, I believe it is critical that we discover "therapist-centered" treatment. In therapist-centered treatment, the therapist understands his spiritual identity and has provided a space in which patients can relate to the entities causing them distress. The therapist also continues to have an ongoing relationship with his soul and the issues that may cause him difficulties. By doing this, we provide a center from which we can guide the treatment process. Native concepts of standing at the center of the cardinal directions provided explanations of therapist-centered treatment for students. The students understood that when they stood at the center of the cardinal points, they were standing in the "seventh sacred direction," which is the center of the universe.

Our elder and great grandfather Black Elk (Neihart, 1959) explained and validated the students' experience of standing in the seventh sacred direction and being able to perceive in a sacred manner. Black Elk was a

Lakota visionary who foresaw the events that would change the way his people would live in the future. Black Elk believed that the center of the universe was everywhere and that all people are at the center, with some actually realizing that they are at the center. Black Elk understood cosmology in a transcendental versus a historical manner.

His teaching explains how any Healer from any tradition can heal if the individual is centered. Centering is the process whereby the Healer is in constant awareness of his own soul's healing process. In this teaching, we understand that there is only one center. This center can be attained by anyone who allows for his awareness to become aware of itself in the seventh sacred direction. In this manner, the Healer can assist the patient in finding her own center of the universe. This is the task of the Healer. This process is completely different from the Western model of pathologizing the patient and making her dependent on a medical model of help to assist her in the life-world.

Needless to say, by the end of the year the students had an identity that transcended the one provided by graduate education. Some students took the time to go to Europe and actually find the "fireplace" or ceremonial place where their ancestors were in touch with their center. This was an experience that not only shaped their lives as therapists but continued to influence them as they traveled through the path of life.

INITIAL SESSIONS

Finally, for therapists and Healers who want to work with these methods of greeting a patient, how one approaches a new encounter is important. I have found that the movement of my body as I walk toward the patient has to be soft, and the walking has to be mindful. Many of my staff over the years have jokingly accused me of lurking or sneaking around because of the way I walk. My practice of martial arts for many years has contributed to this impression. I have found that mindful movement is of key importance in the healing work described in this book. Mindfulness in this work refers to the therapist being completely present in every thought, spoken word, and movement. If the therapist cannot be mindful, the patient will not feel cared for.

Once the patient is approached, great care must be taken during the handshake and when establishing eye contact. Many Native People do not shake hands, but instead merely make contact with the offered hand. This first physical contact is important because the patient will get a "feel" for the ego of the therapist. In addition, eye contact needs to be monitored in case the person comes from a tribe that does not make extended eye contact. The Healer must be able to harmonize with the patient and also get an assessment of acculturation from the patient, depending on how the Healer handles these first few seconds of introduction.

Once the patient is in the office, further introductions are necessary. I usually let the patient know my name and what it is that I do. This does not imply that I identify myself only as a professional. Words like, "I help people in their healing process," are very useful to bring comfort to the patient. I then proceed to ask the patient about his tribe and how connected he is to his people. I ask whether he believes and practices "his ways" and whether he is from a Christian faith. We then proceed to explore some of these beliefs and practices in his life. This exploration will let me know how much of a physical and spiritual support system the client will have during times when therapy may become difficult.

Next I explore the reason that she is seeking help. I ask whether she recalls dreams. If she has had a dream, we work on the interpretation, which will help indicate the direction of the therapy. This is all done in a very low-key and nondirective manner. I explain to the patient that dreams can dictate how the process will unfold. If she does not have dreams to report, we can use other methods such as drawings, sand-tray, imagery, and other nondirective methods. In addition, I let the patient know that prayer is also possible, if she wishes.

Once the problem is verbalized, I try to make the patient aware that problems are not necessarily an indication of pathology. I communicate to the patient that the discomfort he feels could simply be his spirit requiring attention from him and that perhaps certain aspects of his life need to change. I sometimes explain the psychoanalytic model of anxiety and defense mechanisms as an example of how the ego reacts with symptoms, which have deeper causes. (Many Native People, through the acculturation process, have an understanding of the premise on which psychoanalysis is based. One of these basic premises is a hydraulic model in which pressure and release of pressure make for a common-sense understanding.) I explain that most of his suffering is symptomatic and that the suffering cannot be resolved without healing the wound that underlies suffering at the soul level. If the patient is acculturated, I substitute the word *psyche* for *soul*, and I use Western metaphors that all therapists are familiar with to describe the process.

It is critical that the patient is assured that the Healer feels confident in his ability to provide a healing process for the patient. In Traditional Healing circles, the Healer tells the patient that if she does certain things, then healing will occur. An important point here is the understanding that healing does not imply curing or getting rid of all suffering. Healing has to do with being able to harmonize with all that life has to offer. At times, this harmonizing includes being at peace with suffering. It is the relation-ship to the suffering that is important, and the patient can slowly begin to understand that this will change if she continues the treatment. I also let her know during the first session that there may be an indication from a dream or from some other aspect of her person that may reject me as the Healer. In that case, she will have access to another therapist who will har-monize with her psyche and thus give her control of the process.

CHAPTER 4

Historical Trauma:
Treating the Soul Wound

The medicine is already within the pain and suffering. You just
have to look deeply and quietly. Then you realize it has been
there the whole time.

—saying from Native American Oral Tradition

THE CLINICAL APPLICATIONS presented in this chapter will require an open mind to ideas from another worldview. This is critical
since the following discussions will implement some of the theoretical constructs that I have been developing so far. The shifting in metaphor
from the classical Western pathological constructs to Indigenous metaphor in order to maintain cultural competence is critical to this therapeutic
approach. If the intervention provided does not make intuitive sense to
the patient, the treatment will not be effective. In this model of intervention, the spiritual aspects of the life-world become central to the relationship between the Healer and patient. In addition, there must be an actual
understanding of and relationship to the problem or illness afflicting the
patient. In order to form a relationship with a problem or illness, we must
understand that the illness is a conscious entity.

In the case studies that follow, it is assumed that the first few sessions
have occurred and the patient has an understanding of who the therapist is and how the process is unfolding. Some of the problem-solving
mechanisms should be in process, and now it becomes necessary to begin to delve into the source of the patient's problem. By now, a good history should be in place as well as a treatment plan designed to treat the
symptoms and the underlying causes. It is important to note that the case
studies are composite patients in which the therapeutic process has been
"telescoped" in order to present its overall scheme clearly.

In order to gain insight into the historical context of the problem, I
resort to what I have termed over the years "Columbo therapy," named

after the popular television detective who asked the simplest or even stupidest questions in order to solve the case. I have found that trying to ask questions using psychological terminology (termed "psychobabble" by some of my patients) is not very conducive to healing. There are instances where "psychobabble" is appropriate and effective, and the skilled clinician knows when to use it. Some scholars prefer to call this a Freiran approach after the philosophical writing of Paolo Freire (1990), who utilized similar approaches in working with third world communities.

CASE #1:
RECOGNIZING VIOLENCE AS A HISTORICAL INHERITANCE

This patient has been referred for violent behavior. He is not really sure that he wants to be there, but he has become interested in this therapy that appears to be different and unpredictable when compared with his experience with previous therapies. This patient has had a long history of anger and violent behavior, which has resulted in difficulties with the legal system. Alcohol and substance abuse have been part of the problem as he has used these in order to numb the pain that is the driving force behind his anger. After some alliance has been established, I proceed to explore the genesis of the violence in terms of the historical context as understood within a historical trauma paradigm. The dialogue of the case study is presented below and analysis is included following some of the dialogue.

Therapist (T): Where did you learn to be so violent?

> *A stupid Columbo-style question that has never been posed to this patient in the past. At this point I slowly light some sage as a sign to the patient that we are moving into important healing territory that needs to have a spiritual boundary. The use of smoke also can be interpreted through object relations thought in that there is an actual object, which can assist in the catharsis (discharge, cleansing, or releasing) of psychological energy in a manner that is constructive. Therapists who are from a different spiritual tradition may perform a spiritual boundary ritual from their tradition at this time, unless they are firmly grounded in this particular method. This will apply to all other Indigenous practices.*

Patient (P): (*Confused at the simplicity of the question.*) I don't know. I have just been like this.
(T): Is this part of your tribal belief?

Another very stupid question, to which we all know the answer. It is designed to get the patient to start thinking historically and to create some defensive affect. This will enhance critical thinking and questioning of previous beliefs.

(P): No. That is not our way. Our Traditional belief is to respect all life.

(T): How far back in your family has there been violent behavior?

(P): Quite a ways. Grandpa and grandma were violent. I think their parents also were violent. Also, drinking was involved.

(T): So you're saying this isn't part of your tribal tradition, but it seems like it's been there a long time. When do you think this started? I mean if you come from a tribe that respects all life, where did your people learn this from?

Again, this is intended to get the patient to start thinking historically. Most Native People have a good understanding of their tribal history and the type of violence inflicted on their tribe by the colonial process.

(P): Guess it happened when my tribe was almost destroyed by White people. That was a long time ago though, but this is starting to make some sense. Never thought about it like this.

The patient is becoming interested, and the objectivity of history is replacing the guilt of being a "defective Indian," an idea that many Native People have internalized. I want to let the reader know that this has taken a few sessions, and other Western treatment methods, such as supportive, insight, and problem-solving therapy, also are being used.

(T): Violence has an energy to it. Some Traditional beliefs have it that violence is actually a spirit. Spirit can move from place to place and even across the generations. You know, unless someone with "medicine" does something about it.

This is where the therapist needs to be versed in Traditional methods of dealing with spiritual issues. For Christian patients, I utilize Christian metaphor or ideas/stories from the Christian tradition combined with introverted Native affect in order to make the connection to the soul wound or intergenerational trauma. (The reader may think that this is hypocritical on my part since I advise therapists not to dabble in Native spirituality as a technique. I feel that I can do this since I was brought up with Christian teachings and I have integrated these teachings with the teachings of my Original ancestors in a life-long process that continues each day.) I literally will say to the patient that this is the "White way" of understanding this. If the patient is thinking in the White way, I make a point of con-

*veying that there is an "Indian way" of understanding the phenomenon.
In essence, the metaphor of cultural competence is being redefined.*

(P): Wow. I thought that I was just an angry drunk. How come no
one has ever told me about this? (*Patient is realizing that previous
treatment was not culturally competent and served only to pathologize him.*)

(T): Well, most therapists don't know about this stuff either. White
folks would have a problem talking about it cuz it makes them
feel guilty. Lots is being written on this these days, though.
They call it intergenerational trauma, or historical trauma.

(P): You know. I saw something on that on a conference poster.
That's what that was.

*There is hardly a healing conference held in Indian country today in
which historical trauma is not a focus. The notion of the soul wound is
becoming popular and many Native People are aware but have not integrated the knowledge because it's still in the early stages of development
and has not become part of the day-to-day clinical service delivery model.*

(T): Going back to the issue of the violence. Were there any of your
ancestors who went to boarding school? (*Every time I have asked
this question, the patient shows a sadness and seriousness to his affect
that is remarkable.*)

(P): Yes, my parents and their parents. They went to boarding
school back east. They were caught and sent to that school
against their will.

(T): What do you think happened there? How were they treated?

*Again a stupid question, since it is common knowledge how widespread
the abuse was in these institutions. Violence took the form of prohibition
of Native language, religion, dress, or anything else that might be used
as a form of cultural identity. In addition, there was a very high rate of
physical and sexual abuse in these boarding schools. This sets up the process for understanding internalized oppression as described previously.*

(P): They were beaten. Beaten just for being Indians. For speaking our language. For praying to our Creator in our way. They
were raped sometimes. (*Patient is usually very sad at the recollection of history. Anger also is manifested.*)

(T): Yes, this is true. So, you can start seeing where your anger
started. How it was passed on down to you. You see, this puts
you in a very powerful place right now. You can heal your
great grandparents, your parents, and all the way up the line.

You also can heal all of your children and their children by healing yourself. You see, this is the only place that the ancestors can heal their soul wound. They didn't have the opportunity to heal when they were alive, so the energy of the anger was passed on down. Now that you understand, you can bring a lot of "medicine" to your family and tribe.

This is an existential moment for the patient in which his personal anger and sadness are given a special power to heal what means the most to him. Therefore, we are turning suffering into healing. I also explain the notion of internalized oppression and the vampire image, which was discussed earlier. At this point, I light some sweet-grass and offer the lit braid to the patient, who takes the smoking braid and blesses himself as a symbol of connectedness to the ancestors and to all creation. This ceremonial act also allows the patient to know that whatever entities were invoked in the discussion are now appeased and he can have peace outside of the session. I instruct the patient that in no circumstances is he to do his own therapy at this point in time. But many patients become very interested in the process and want to continue on their own or with friends. This could be a dangerous practice, which could exacerbate their symptoms. The reason this could be dangerous is that patients may begin to delve into areas of their trauma without a therapeutic boundary, which is critical to gaining the insight that will help them overcome the trauma. I impress upon them that I have been doing this for a long time and have a sense of the risks. This request is made to facilitate healing, not merely for control over the patient. In time, patients will be able to navigate these waters on their own, when they have acquired enough strength, ego integrity, and skills in this area.

Acknowledging Intergenerational Issues

During the sessions, the patient usually brings in dream material that indicates that there is an intergenerational process occurring. Dreams in which parents and other ancestors bring the patient gifts are common. The patient realizes that the therapy is occurring at another level, which enhances the patient's interest in the process. It is no longer just a therapeutic theory or technique. The patient is deeply immersed in a deep healing process that involves the generations.

Non-Native therapists can guide this process, with some needed modifications. If non-Native therapists are willing to deal with the soul wound, they also will have to be willing to acknowledge their role in a historical context. I have advised interns over the years to never, never try to disavow complicity by saying things like, "I wasn't there," or "That's in the past." One of the worst things that non-Native therapists can do is to compare their historical trauma with the Native one. Of course, other cultures have historical trauma. But this process is about the patient and not the therapist. Such comparison will invalidate the patient's trauma and end the open healing process. Instead, non-Native therapists should acknowledge, in an honest and direct way, the role of their ancestors in causing the trauma. This enhances the therapeutic alliance because it is based on honesty. Honesty is always a good thing, especially in the healing circle.

Years ago I told one intern, who happened to have blue eyes, to acknowledge this in the session. She was having difficulty connecting with the patient. I told her to ask the patient what he saw when he looked into her blue eyes. I had her ask the patient if perhaps he did not see Custer's eyes when he looked into her eyes. This acknowledgment propelled the therapy into a process that I could not have imagined. From that point on, the patient was able to disclose even the most well-guarded secrets to the therapist. Of course, this took a lot of courage, but Healers must have courage. Otherwise, they should become bankers or enter some other profession. I have told the therapists whom I have supervised over the years that as Healers we are not "civilians" and we are to be held to a higher standard. Also, not being civilians implies a certain warrior personality that is the key to the work that must be accomplished.

Assessing and Working with Typology

Even as these complex interactions are occurring, the therapist also needs to make an assessment of the type of typology that the patient is manifesting. It is best to keep this simple and stay with the basic types that Jung (1971) described in his monumental treatise on this subject. The main reason for understanding typology is that, in keeping with Traditional Healing, it is critical that balance be restored. After all, most Traditional systems hold the belief that the loss of harmony and balance is at the core of symptom manifestation.

Initially the therapist should assess the dominant type that the patient presents with. The assessment process can be accomplished through the therapeutic relationship if the therapist is familiar with the theoretical nuances of typology. Therapists who are not familiar with typology can refer to standardized assessments that may assist in this process.

Typology can be explained through the psychological definitions given by Jung as well as through Native understanding of the six cardinal points. The following brief descriptions should give readers basic knowledge that will assist them in understanding the case studies:

- There are six cardinal directions from which the life-world can be understood: the west, north, east, south, sky, and earth. Jung's six psychological functions—thinking, feeling, intuition, sensation, introversion, and extraversion—can be represented in these cardinal points (a detailed description of the Native/Jungian typology can be found in Duran & Duran, 1995). The person who walks in balance is at the center of the six points. This is known as the seventh sacred direction. (In the Western understanding of typology, Jung's six psychological functions are not static, and the task for psychological balance is to literally be at the center where no one type dominates. The different combinations of types makes the task both interesting and challenging.)
- When working with the directions or types, the Healer/therapist needs to first understand where the imbalance exists. Once this determination has been made, therapy/healing and/or ceremony may be used to bring the patient back to the center, or the seventh sacred direction.
- It is important to note that when the patient is moving from his strong direction or type into a lesser used or "inferior function," new issues can emerge. The patient will find that there is negative psychological material or shadow beneath the inferior function. Therefore, the Healer must be especially mindful while guiding the patient through the balancing process. Symptoms such as sadness or depression are common when the patient moves into a lesser known area or inferior function.

As the Healer/therapist begins to understand how the patient functions, the therapist can begin to treat the inferior function, or function opposite the predominant function. (For example, if thinking predominates, then feeling would be the inferior function.) If the patient is predominantly a thinking type, balance must be restored by enhancing the feeling function. I attempt to do this by keeping the therapeutic work in the inferior function as much as possible or comfortable for the patient. In other words, with a thinking-type personality, the therapist will have to use language that is not linear or logical and has more of an intuitive, feeling quality. In the beginning, this creates confusion and discomfort for the patient, who will gravitate toward experience that is comfortable within the thinking function. (This is a very brief introduction into typology due to the scope of the present work. The reader is encouraged to read Jung's *Psychological Types* [1971] for more in-depth study.)

The therapist has to balance the extraversion and introversion function depending on the typology of the patient. If the patient is extraverted, the energy of the session needs to be balanced by making it more introverted, and vice versa. As the reader can see by now, this requires a tremendous amount of mindfulness and attention to the smallest details within the healing encounter. As the therapy progresses, the patient will be educated regarding the intent of the balancing act so it can be integrated into conscious awareness of the process. Conscious integration also will enhance trust in the therapist's capabilities because the patient will realize that the therapist has been devoting complete mindfulness to the treatment process.

CASE #2:
WORKING WITH THE FEELING FUNCTION

In this case, the thinking or analytic function is keeping the patient from living in balance because he analyzes and deconstructs most of his relationships in the life-world. This approach to life does not usually bring happiness, and the patient often presents with dysthymic symptoms consistent with existential angst (an overall sadness about life due to loss of meaning). Dissatisfaction with life also can make the patient prone to escapist behaviors such as drug and alcohol abuse and possible addiction.

(T): You are thinking too much.

(P): What do you mean? How else am I going to understand?

(T): What is it you want to understand? If it was up to your head knowing, you wouldn't be here talking to me in the first place. You're smart enough to figure out this stuff on your own.

(P): Yah, but I'm not feeling so good. (*Patient has used a feeling metaphor, which opens the door to deal with feeling from the heart.*)

(T): How do you know? (*This is a Columbo question that will sidetrack the analytic function of this very intelligent patient.*)

(P): How do I know what?

(T): That you're not feeling so good?

(P): Well, I get sad and anxious. I can't sleep, and I worry.

(T): Is that happening in your head?

(P): Hmmm. . . . that's a good question. (*Further confusion because his analytic function is not able to reach into this feeling realm.*)

(T): Well, where is it then? You know the sadness? Is it in your little finger? (*A very stupid question that is intended to cause the patient get in touch with his body.*)

(P): Of course not. (*Moment of silence as patient starts to search for the feeling. This is the first time he is scanning his body.*)

(T): Did you find it yet? Is it here, or here, or here? (*I point to differ-ent parts of my abdomen and heart area.*)

(P): Kinda in here. (*Pointing to area just under his heart.*)

(T): Sounds like you need to move out of your head a little more, eh?

(P): How do you do that?

(T): I'm going to tell you, but you are probably not going to believe me since it's so simple. (*I stay silent for a moment and wait for in-terest to build.*)

(P): Yah? Well, try me anyway. I can check it out.

(T): You have to get in touch with the howl.

> *Most Native patients are familiar with Coyote stories and the power be-hind this spirit. This is a profoundly ridiculous request on my part that cannot be figured out, even by the most intelligent analytic patients. I say this in order to allow the patient to experience confusion and lose some of the control that has not been very helpful in his life. Of course, control can be useful. The patient needs to learn the useful versus the nonuseful aspects of being in control with his thinking function and leaving the feeling function out.*

(P): What? (*Obviously confused and in disbelief thinking that he mis-heard what I said about the howl.*)

(T): You heard me. I know you did. I said, "howl."

(P): That's what I thought you said. You are kidding of course.

(T): No. I'm not kidding.

> *At this point, the therapy has shifted from an ego point of view to a transpersonal one. The patient is no longer controlling with his analytic function. He is uncomfortable because this is new emotional territory and he has moved into the inferior function. He hasn't had much experience here, and he doesn't know what to do.*

(P): Are you going to explain this? (*The patient is struggling to bring the therapy back to the analytic function because that is his strength. It is also the reason for his lack of psychological balance.*)

(T): If I could, I would. This has to be realized within the howl itself. (*This is frustrating to the patient because now he has to do something in order to began differentiating the inferior function.*)

(P): Exactly how am I supposed to do this?

(T): Simple. I won't ask you to do it here because you're not ready. When you're in your car or somewhere where no one can hear you, I want you to howl from the depth of your gut.

(P): You are kidding me. What does this have to do with therapy? I can't do that. That's way embarrassing.

(T): You asked, so I'm telling you. You have to howl. In that howl, you will find all of creation. Okay, we have done enough today.

I light sweet-grass as an offering to the healing spirits and to let the patient see that even this most ridiculous request is contained in a spiritual boundary. Some patients have taken up to 6 months before they actually can howl in total secrecy and usually it's what I call a "wimpy howl." In time, they start to realize that not all is accessible to understanding from the thinking function.

The intervention is reversed if the patient is operating from a feeling/intuitive approach. My task in this case would be to offer interventions to take the patient into the inferior function, which would be the thinking function. I would reverse the metaphors. I would ask the patient to do thinking tasks that would make him as uncomfortable in the undifferentiated thinking function as the patient in this case is with the feeling realm.

CONCLUSION

In this chapter I have introduced the practical use of some of the theoretical ideas discussed previously. There is a lot of material in these cases, which presumes that the therapist has a background in areas such as typology and other Jungian theory. It is not the intent in this book to rewrite the contributions of Jung, Freud, or other theorists. Most graduate courses in the disciplines involved in therapy work have a history and systems requirement in which most of these theories are discussed in detail.

Regarding the case study in typology, I am compelled to discuss some of my own process in this area. I had to move into the thinking/extraverted function in order to find balance since I'm predominantly an introverted/intuitive type. A dream I had while I was working on my dissertation reveals the nature of this balancing struggle: In the dream the chair of my dissertation committee was punching me on the left temporal area of my head. It is clear that my logical processing function was being tortured because I was being forced into this area by the very rational dissertation process. The suffering that I was encountering at the time was well depicted by the dream. Symptoms of depression and anxiety were also present. Once that area of my life became more balanced by my being able to operate in the thinking arena, the symptoms subsided. Of course, the strong functions remain a sort of "home base" until the inferior functions are fully differentiated and fluidity allows one to move into whatever psychological function is required by any given situation. The task of full differentiation is life-long, of course, and in no way am I pretending to be there yet.

Treatment becomes increasingly complex at this point because all of the different facets of Western approaches are being utilized along with Indigenous clinical methods. Therapists need to remain focused and centered during this process in order to maintain harmony and balance in the session. Fluidity between the worldviews is necessary if the therapeutic encounter is going to be culturally competent and useful.

CHAPTER 5

The Spirit of Alcohol:
Treating Addiction

In the Tibetan Book of the Dead, Indian holy man Padmasambha-va describes how we must face energies that appear as wrathful entities: "The wrathful deities represent hope, and the peaceful deities represent fear. Fear in the sense of irritation, because the ego cannot manipulate them in any way; they are utterly invincible, they never fight back. The hopeful quality of wrathful energy is hope in the sense of a perpetual creative situation, seen as it really is, as basic neutral energy which constantly exists, belonging to neither good nor bad." (Trungpa, 1975, p. 26)

TREATMENT IDEAS discussed in this and the next few chapters had their genesis in the training that I received from my "Root Teacher" Tarrence. During my time in graduate school, I was fortunate to have had a parallel training program through the teachings of this holy man. I introduce this chapter with an exchange that we had regarding the topic of addiction. Further writings describing this relationship with Tarrence are found in my book *Buddha in Redface* (2000).

TEACHINGS ON THE SPIRIT OF ALCOHOL

During my training with Tarrence, we talked about the meaning of addictions. He was very interested in what I was learning about addictions as part of my doctoral training. Tarrence also wanted to know what was going on with my clinical work. I told him about a strange experience I had working with substance abuse patients in which the patients related to alcohol as a living energy. At the time I believed that addictions were mostly as described in Western psychological theory. My thinking of not just addictions, but also psychopathology, was to be conflicted and transformed. Part of the conversation we had was as follows (Duran, 2000):

"The last couple of times I worked with people at the clinic, the drinkers, you know—well, I had the distinct feeling that something was watching or that there was something more to the addiction. I noticed that the patients were feeling as if the addiction was not simply a problem. Instead, the addiction had a feeling of being alive and characteristics of an intelligent being."

"Exactly what do you think alcoholism, or any addiction, is?"

I gave him the best textbook definition of addiction I had. I pulled out all the stops and let him know about the biochemical, psychological, and family-dynamic aspects of alcoholism and addiction: everything I knew. I gave a detailed explanation that I thought was nothing short of brilliant. When I finished, Tarrence laughed even harder. This threw me off guard since I thought my talk had been quite eloquent.

"What's so funny? I really don't see that I made any jokes about any of this," I complained. "What do you think it is then?"

"Medicine," he said in a serious tone.

"Medicine? You mean like for medicinal purposes?"

"No, as in medicine. As in Indian medicine. As in dreamtime medicine. Spirit, that's what I'm saying."

I was skeptical. "Can you explain a little more?"

"All of those drugs, alcohol, and all that, come from life itself, from the Earth awareness. Since they come from the Earth awareness, they have life and duality. All of those substances can be used for good or not. Your patients have activated the negative side of medicine. Once they activate the negative side of medicine, then there's a price to pay.

"You see, there's a contract between the medicine—alcohol or whatever—and the person taking it. It is its own ceremony. The person wants to have a different experience in the dream (many elders use the word *dream* to depict the life-world). The alcohol says OK, and the deal is made. Except that usually the person drinking is too ignorant to know that he or she has to make good with the deal. Once someone drinks it, then the spirit of alcohol waits for the time when it can take its due. Since it is spirit, it wants spirit in return. Therefore, it takes someone's life. The whole time all this is done, the spirit is further disrespected by people treating it like an addiction or whatnot.

"This is for real, and you know the stats. How many thousands of our relatives has this medicine taken? This is part of the price for the action the dreamers did. In their ignorance and grief, they gave over many people and much suffering—much the same way present-day alcoholics do. They sell their own spirit for a brief spell in their grief and suffering, not realizing the long-term cause and effect they activate. But again, this was part of the deal," Tarrence said with sadness in his eyes.

"Makes sense. I mean, the feeling I've been getting. It's real. I knew it was some sort of entity looking at me. I knew there was awareness. But I didn't realize the implications of all this. You're saying that all the suffering by our people, and all the dying through alcoholism, is for the purpose of changing the karma planted by the owl dreamers (a type of dreamer that has access to the underworld or the unconscious and can operate in a dreamtime awareness or an awareness that is available to Shamans)."

"Yes. As you can see, our actions have profound implications. That's why the Buddha gave us such simple tools for living. If we followed those, then we wouldn't have to worry about all this. Also, the stuff that you know, you already knew. You need to start trusting that knowing," Tarrence said.

"So any ideas about how to deal with it?" I asked, knowing that he knew exactly what to do.

"Ceremony."

"Ceremony?" I parroted.

"Since the person activates the spirit of alcohol in a ceremony, then it makes sense that the spirit and the relationship with it must also be dealt with in ceremony. What you do—therapy—that's a ceremony. So you already have the makings of what to do. You just need to be honest with what you're doing. Have your patients enact a ceremony that changes the relationship with the spirit of alcohol. They must acknowledge it. They must talk to it. Once they talk to it, they establish a different relationship with it. Now they can make a deal with it. They can give it some other type of spiritual gift, like tobacco. Tobacco was put here by the awareness for just such things. The spirit of alcohol will take the offering since it's offered in a respectful manner, and the person's spirit will be safe within this new ceremony."

"Makes sense. I guess I could call it active imagination. The tobacco can be the transitional object. . . . Yeah, this can work," I said.

"Call it whatever you want. As long as you know that you're conducting a serious life-and-death ritual with your patient," Tarrence asserted sternly.

ADDICTION AS A SPIRITUAL DISORDER

As a graduate student, I found that Tarrence's thoughts regarding alcoholism were similar to those expressed by Carl Jung (Adler, 1984). In a series of letters to Bill W. the well-known founder of Alcoholics Anonymous (A.A.), Jung described alcoholism as a state of possession (Adler, 1984; www.rewritables.net/cybriety/the_billw-_carl_jun_letters.htm).   These letters reveal the deep connection that AA has to the notion of alcohol as a "spirit" very much in the same manner that Tarrence explained in the above passage. There are more similarities in the way that the psyche understands these phenomena than we are led to believe by the contemporary systems of thought that have been so widely accepted in the treatment of addictions. This is illustrated in the correspondence between Jung and Bill W.

In his letters, Bill W. clearly expresses his thoughts and feelings regarding alcoholism and his own struggle with the addiction to alcohol. He makes mention of Roland H. (a pioneer with Bill W. in the A.A. movement), who became Jung's patient after exhausting all other possible treatments for his addiction, with no relief. The intervention that made the most sense to Roland H. and to Bill W. was the honesty that Jung displayed in his response to the situation. Basically, Jung agreed with Roland H. that further psychiatric treatment was hopeless, and the only possible hope would be some type of religious experience. Bill W. goes on to tell Jung that he himself had become severely addicted to alcohol and was quite hopeless about recovering. In this desperate state of addiction and depression, Bill W. realized that he needed to cry out to a "higher power." According to the A.A. tradition, his release from the addiction was immediate (Bill W., 2005).

In his response to Bill W., Jung stressed that he should be very careful in what he said to Roland H. because Jung was already being misunderstood by most of the Western psychological world. Jung makes the point in his letter to Bill W. that the craving for alcohol is the equivalent of a spiritual thirst for wholeness that can best be exemplified by the medieval image of a union with God. Jung continues by making the point that the Latin word for spirit, "spiritus," by which alcohol also is known, is the word for religious experience. In addition, Jung tells Bill W. that there is an evil principle that prevails in the world that an ordinary individual cannot resist unless there is some protection from a higher source of power.

It is apparent that Jung has shifted the metaphor of addiction from the Western medical model to a spiritual context. He is careful not to divulge too much regarding spiritual interventions, perhaps in fear of criticism or invalidation of his work. In writing this book, I have felt similar trepidation. However, I feel that the time is right to recover what has been lost of our soul. In essence, I am trying to bring the soul back into the healing container or therapeutic office.

It is clear from the interactions between myself and Tarrence, and between Bill W. and Jung, that we are dealing in a totally different epistemology from the Western medical model. Calling the relationships "crosscultural" would only cheapen the profound wisdom and compassion contained in such honest understanding. The insight given in such meetings has become the cornerstone of the work that I do.

In the correspondence between Jung and Bill W. we can see parallels in the conceptualization of addiction in Jung's mind and the description given by my teacher Tarrence. These similarities are helpful in facilitating the shift of metaphors in the minds of modern Western-trained therapists. Basically, I am presenting this material in order to bring "face validity" to the clinical case material that follows in the next few chapters. If the soul metaphor was an accepted paradigm in our profession, this would not be necessary.

ALCOHOLIC AS A NAME

Many of the patients I have dealt with for many years have presented with addictions issues. For the most part, they identify themselves by the label given to them in a naming ceremony by some type of healer. Many patients identify themselves as an "alcoholic/addict" even before they give their names. When they do this, the first thing I do is to ask what name their mother or grandparents call them. This is the first step in undoing the naming ceremony that was begun by some other healer or sorcerer. This renaming is also the beginning of a decolonizing process that has deep roots in the psyche of the individual and community.

Interventions in this area involve all of the aforementioned material in a mercurial intertwining with the notions of the spirit of alcohol or drug of choice. The therapist needs to have a firm understanding and ability to implement Western treatment as well as the treatments mentioned here as part of this hybrid approach. Therapists must have an understanding of historical trauma and the impact it has had on Native people. They also must have knowledge of the spiritual issues discussed by Jung in his letters with Bill W. and the notions described in the conversation with Tarrence. Most Native patients have an intuitive understanding of these ideas, but in the beginning this idea of the spirit of drugs may make them uncomfortable. The fact that so many patients have been in many recovery programs calls for an approach that can entertain and confuse the patient. Attempting to discuss addiction in the usual manner with these patients will not be effective because they already know more than we do and their defenses have been well honed by their experience with previous therapists/sorcerers.

You may find it remarkable that I am classifying therapists with sorcerers. There is a fine line between the Healer who heals and the one who, due to ignorance, may cause harm. In working with patients, I have found that archaic language and images are the best means of relating to the spirit or the unconscious. Referring to an ignorant therapist as a "practitioner of iatrogenic illness" would evoke little feeling in the patient and there would be no affective connection to the healer/therapist. Therefore, I use the word *sorcerer* in order to make the point about the seriousness of some of the actions taken by therapists toward patients. This affective connection is crucial to the task of allowing the soul to open to the process of healing.

My understanding from the teachings of Tarrence is that when the soul is wounded it goes back into the "black world" (unconscious). Psychological regression occurs. This regression makes a huge spiritual gap in the person who has been wounded. Because natural law dictates that soul or spirit seeks itself, it follows that the person begins to seek "spirit." Given that the true nature of the person is regressed, the only access to soul is through the ego. Ego is hardly equipped for this task because ego is conditioned by experience and results from what the person has learned. It is interesting that ego makes an attempt to find spirit and, with its pitiful insight, finds material spirit, the spirit in the bottle.

Before you get "weirded out," let me suggest that the next time you go to a restaurant, look at the back page of the menu. In the beverage section, you will find the most curious beverage. Under a section labeled "spirits" you will be able to purchase your favorite spirit or drink. In therapy, patients are educated about this because they find these ideas preposterous at times too. Also, you can find advertisements for spirits in bright neon at any of your favorite taverns or sports bars across the country. I will ask a stupid Columbo-type question, "Why do they call it spirit?"

When the patient is in search of spirit to replace the spiritual and existential emptiness caused by the soul wound, ego (the aspect of the personality in which the personal identity and experience is accessible) projects into the spirit of alcohol. The spirit of alcohol then is introjected by ego and consumed by the person in its physical form. This gives the essence of the alcohol a curious quality of being alive, which is best described by Levi-Strauss (1958) as a process of complete participation with the world. In essence, this process involves unconscious projection into the world and at the same time introjecting the content of the individual's own projection back into ego awareness. This gives the world a "live" quality. Of course, this description is anthropological, and the Native person sees the object as being alive in and of itself. This is important when viewed from the perspective that the soul-wounding process has left a spiritual emptiness in the person who is addicted. In essence, the person is replacing spirit with alcohol spirit in an attempt to fill the void created by historical trauma.

The person then has the illusion that rather than being of spirit she is full of rapture. In someone who has consumed alcohol spirits, this illusion of rapture continues to fool the ego. The ego accepts that there is fullness of true spirit. In a short time, the physical consequences of addiction begin to complicate the life of the individual. At this point, it does not matter as much why the person has to continue drinking. The spirit in the bottle has taken possession of the person at the physical, psychological, and spiritual levels. Once addiction occurs, its symptoms need to be treated in order to treat the underlying soul wound.

By failing to deal with addiction as described here, Western treatment approaches fall short with Native and other patients. It is little wonder that addiction continues to be a problem to society as a whole and that countless lives are lost each year despite many attempts to treat this as a simple pathology. Native patients have responded with understanding to these ideas over the years, in both individual as well as group settings. In order to address the addiction, patients must learn about the relationship at the spiritual level. Then, they can begin to implement some of these ideas in their daily life as they work on healing the soul wound. The approach is not to lead them away from alcohol. My approach has been one of realizing the relationship to the spirit of alcohol and engaging in that relationship with full consciousness and insight.

I want to make it clear that some patients do recover in treatment using Western methods such as A.A. and other models. However, some patients are seeking meaning as well as sobriety. What is critical in the work described here is that in addition to recovering from addiction, the patient also may want to have an existential reconnection with who they are as a Native person. It is a good thing to be sober. I believe that it also can be a good thing to be sober and to have an understanding of who you are in the greater context of being in the life-world. The material discussed in this section on treatment addresses both goals: that is, recovery that also has existential meaning.

CASE #3:
RELATING TO THE SPIRIT OF ALCOHOL

In the following case, I describe the treatment process as it unfolds in the early sessions of working on addiction or the relationship with these "spirits." In the process of treatment, the patient brings in dream material from session to session that usually lets him know that he is involved in a spiritual situation. Relationship with spirit is established through the process of offerings, or transitional objects that the essence of the spirit of alcohol or drug will accept in exchange for the patient's healing. The dreams of the Healer are also important in this process because the Healer must be willing to travel into the "underworld" and assist the patient in the journey through the black world of the unconscious as the patient searches for what has been lost through the soul wound.

The inability of our profession to deal with the reality of the Native patient is illustrated by an exchange I had with a Shaman early in my training as a psychologist. He told me, "The difference between what I do and what you do is simple. You take patients all the way to the edge of the cliff and you leave them standing there. I push them over, and I go with them into the abyss. Then I bring them back. That's the difference" (Bill W., personal communication, May 4, 1985). I am not suggesting that Western therapists should push their patients over the abyss. Instead, we should be cognizant that there are other levels to treatment and we should continue honing our skills in order to be able to take patients where they need to go. It is difficult to understand this idea without a case study. Therefore, we will proceed to clinical case material. The patient is a man in his 40s who has had several attempts at treatment for alcoholism. He also has underlying problems such as sadness, anger, unresolved grief, and historical trauma, which continue to fuel the symptoms of alcoholism.

(T): What's going on?
(P): I'm an alcoholic.
(T): How do you know?

> *This question begins to deconstruct the pathological model of the patient's colonized worldview. Not only will the patient be on his way to another way of thinking or being in the life-world, but he will be gaining a connection to his Traditional belief system, which will allow him to regain his existential meaning. Loss of this meaning and identity in the colonizing process is part of the problem.*

(P): Well, I'm not in denial. I've been to A.A. and treatment before. I know that this is a disease that is progressive.

> *Patients usually parrot what they have heard. They believe that this is what the Healer wants to hear; otherwise they will be accused of yet another pathology, that is, denial. This intervention involves keeping the patient sober in the present as well as addressing underlying causes of addiction in order to foster a long-term sober lifestyle. We don't want to take away an intervention that can help, such as A.A. We also don't want to keep the patient unconscious of what is occurring at the spiritual level.*

(T): Sounds like you know more than I do about that.

This suggestion sets the stage to have the patient see himself as an equal in the process of healing and continues to deconstruct his colonized worldview. This focusing of attention on the process will allow the patient to be an expert in the process and will help him to continue having awareness of his life-world.

(P): Well, I have been in a few treatment programs and I have studied the A.A. Big Book.

(T): Big Book. That's good. Do they have a little book? (*It's important to use humor. In this case I'm letting the patient know that not all that is written is necessarily true for him. The humor helps keep defensiveness about A.A. to a minimum.*)

(P): You know, it's all in there. The steps.

(T): How far are you in the steps? That first one is a gnarly one. Man, if I could just understand step one, I'd really know something. That Bill W. was something else.

This validates A.A. and moves the discussion toward the spirit of alcohol. By looking deeply into step one (step one is where individuals understand and accept that they are powerless over alcohol and they need to resort to a power higher than themselves if they are to recover), it's not a far stretch to help the patient gain insight into the spiritual relationship with alcohol, much in the manner that Jung helped Bill W. gain insight into his addictive process.

(P): Yah. Step one took me a while. There's a lot there.

(T): What do you think that might mean in the Indian way?

This helps me assess how much acculturation there is and to launch the "spiritus mercurius" or the relationship to alcohol that is crucial to the decolonizing intervention. The patient also will realize that there are parallel ways of thinking that don't necessarily exclude each other.

(P): Well, I know the elders have a lot to say about it. It's a White man's illness. They say that I should get White man's medicine for it.

(T): Do you believe like that?

This is a sensitive issue. Questioning the elders can be very insulting. At this point, I also let the patient know that much of what is considered Traditional may in actuality be Western, given that colonization goes back 500 years. I explain to the patient that the oldest elder may be in his 80s. This would mean that his grandparents lived about 150 years ago. By that time in history, Native People had already been colonized for at least 300 years. Therefore, what is considered ancient knowledge very well may be contaminated with Western ideology. This also introduces the patient to the historical trauma issue, as discussed previously.

(P): Well yah, I believe them. But then, there are a lot of elders who drink. It's hard to know what to believe.

(T): Can I tell you something? The way it was explained to me by a holy man?

With this introduction, there is no way that the patient will say no. That I acquired this information from a holy man gets attention and respect. At this point, I will burn sage or sweet-grass in order to let the patient know we are moving into sacred turf and we need a spiritual boundary.

(P): Yes. I have respect for the holy ones.

(T): I was told that alcohol, and all drugs for that matter, are medicine. You know, medicine in the Indian way.

This lets patient know that the metaphor has changed. Medicine now has an Indian meaning, which places the discussion into an even deeper sacred place.

(P): Medicine? Never heard it like that.

(T): You see, when they make alcohol they use all the sacred elements. It's life that is being transformed from grapes or whatnot. Air, fire, water, and earth are used. That's what you are made of also, so it knows you. Since it is sacred it has a dual aspect. Depending on how you use it, the medicine will respond to you. Since it's medicine, it should be used only by those who know medicine, like medicine people. If you're not a medicine person, you should leave it alone. If you use it anyway, then you are the opposite. Do you know what is the opposite of a medicine person?

(P): A witch or a sorcerer.

This question is always answered in a manner that indicates that the patient has knowledge of the dual nature of healing. This also will become very disturbing to patients as they begin to integrate the meaning of this fact.

(T): Yes. When you use this medicine this way, you are doing sorcery on yourself and your loved ones. It's very scary stuff. I wonder sometimes why people do this. I take it you're not a medicine person? (*I ask this in order to let patients know that they have been performing sorcery on themselves and their families.*) Every time you use this medicine, you are taking a big risk. Amazing though. The same medicine can be the "Blood of

Christ" or sorcery. Interesting, eh? (*This shows the patient that intentionality and consciousness are very critical.*)

(P): Sounds pretty heavy when you say it like that.

(T): It is heavy. You know there is a contract that happens between your spirit and the spirit of alcohol. Spirit knows spirit, and they know the etiquette of spirit even if you don't.

(P): What do you mean?

(T): When you approach the spirit in the bottle, your spirit recognizes it and the alcohol spirit recognizes your spirit. They enter an agreement. The alcohol spirit lets your spirit know that it will give you something. It can be relief, laughter, sleep, or whatever. Then, your spirit agrees to give something back. What do you think the alcohol spirit wants?

(P): I don't know. Hard to tell.

Most patients are very uncomfortable with where this is going. Also, I must remind the reader that this intervention may take several sessions depending on the dreams that the patient is having and how much the patient's ego can tolerate.

(T): Well, because it's spirit it can want only one thing. That is spirit. Your spirit (*pointing at the patient*). It could make an exchange, though, and it could want the spirit of someone in your family.

This is extremely powerful because most Native patients have lost loved ones to alcoholism. The fact that they have lost loved ones gives this point an especially valid energy, and some guilt can arise. If a lot of guilt is expressed, this is a good spot in the process to discuss the historical trauma issues and how alcohol was systematically introduced into Native communities in order to steal the land.

(P): Never thought of it like that. How come they didn't tell me this when I was in treatment?

(T): They really don't know about this stuff. Actually, if they heard me tell you this stuff they would think I was crazy. (*This helps the therapeutic alliance. If I'm on the margins, this places me closer to the patient than to the profession. Here I insert some humor that has a lot of truth.*)

(P): Guess they would. You're not like a real psychologist. At least not like any that I've had. (*In the scenario that follows there is a lot of Indigenous metaphor that relates to Traditional Healing etiquette.*)

(T): You know, when you drink or use drugs, it is a ceremony? Let me explain this to you.

(P): O.K. Let me hear this.

(T): When you go to your church, which is really called a bar, you enter from the east door. (*Of course not all bars have doors facing east, but here I say this to make a Traditional Healing metaphor. This will help the patient understand the sorcery activity and the dual nature of "medicine."*) When you go in, there's already a congregation in there. Some are singing, some are dancing, and so on. In front, there is a huge altar, called "the bar." Behind this altar, is a priest of some sort called a "bartender." I don't think he's a good medicine person, so this would make him a sorcerer. You step up to the bar, leave your token just like when you go to a medicine person you give him tobacco or a gift, and request the kind of medicine you want. Same here. You place a token of money and request your medicine. You know, there's even a secret sorcerer's language spoken here. Anywhere else in the country, if you ask someone for a screwdriver, they will hand you a tool. Here screwdriver means a type of medicine. The sorcerer proceeds to pour different types of spirit into your container. He then shakes it to the four directions. (*I make a shaking motion to the directions. Usually, this brings laughter of a serious type, because it is too true for comfort.*) Then you proceed to drink this. You have completed your ceremony. Now, the contract is in place. The medicine will give you what you want. It will keep its part of the bargain. Now it will be up to you to fulfill your part.

(P): It sounds really serious when you talk about it like that. It sounds hopeless. I mean I already did these ceremonies to the spirit of alcohol. I can't undo that. What do I do?

The patient is worried about more than just his drinking addiction. This has placed the therapy at a new level, where patients are ready to explore Traditional interventions that not only will address the addiction but also will connect them back to their existential humanity. They are ready to reconnect with their ancestors and become who they are. This is a very liberating phase and most patients are grateful to begin to experience their "soul" becoming intact.

(T): There are ways. In the spirit world, it's all about etiquette and manners. So far, you have forgotten these. All traditions have manners when it comes to dealing with these forces.

At this point, I reiterate the story in the New Testament (Holy Bible, Mark chapter 5, verses 1–20) about when Christ came into contact with the possessed man. I make a point of indicating the manners, and I add humor to the story. For instance, I take the language into modern "hip" language and out of the King James style to make points such as: "The Christ says, 'What's going on bro.?' The demons then respond, 'not much, just chilln.' Christ answers, 'Well, I would really rather you don't torture this bro. anymore.' 'Well, what you got to offer as trade?'" This is a critical part of the story because now the point can be made that there are deals that can be made or changed in the spiritual realm. This will facilitate belief by patients that they also can undo their contracts with the spirit of alcohol.

(P): You know, I remember that story, but no one ever told it like that.

(T): Well, you know Christ wasn't an uptight kind of fellow. I think he knew how to go with the flow. Since you want to let go of the spirit of alcohol, you need to talk to it and ask what it wants in exchange for your spirit. I'm sure you can work out a deal.

In my office, I have a "fetish" representing the spirit of alcohol. Fetishes usually are made of stone and symbolize the essence of the animal, plant, or whatever else they represent. The fetish I use is shaped and looks exactly like a bottle of Dark Eyes vodka, which is a cheap, high alcohol content drink. At this point I bring this into the center of the session.

(T): Here is my friend (*I point to Dark Eyes, and the patient usually becomes anxious*). We can talk to it now. Actually, he's been hearing every word we've been saying. Dark Eyes is already wondering if you're going to have manners. You know as part of your step four through step eight that you also need to make amends to the medicine here.

I'm making reference to the A.A. model in which one has to take a fearless inventory that ends with the person actually making amends to those people that have been hurt in the process of the person's being addicted. In this intervention, I have the patient make amends to the spirit of alcohol in a manner that changes the relationship to alcohol from aversion to one that does not make the person fearful. I am not advocating drinking alcohol. I am trying to get the patient to relate to the energy of alcohol and addiction in a mindful way that will allow the patient to remain free of the addiction and to be able to deal with the cravings, if they arise, as part of the ongoing relationship to the spirit of alcohol.

(P): How do I do that? What do I say?

(T): When you make an offering, you know what to do. You can offer tobacco, cornmeal, food, water, and such. It's the intent that is important, and the spirit of alcohol will recognize the honesty of your spirit as you go into this new way of relating with awareness.

(P): I don't have anything on me to give now.

(T): Man, what kinda Indian are you? You're out there in the world with no protection.

Jokingly I say this but making a point that shows the patient how disconnected he is. I open a drawer where I keep tobacco, cornmeal, and such. I hand the patient one of these. I motion for the patient to leave an offering on the fetish with the intent that the spirit of alcohol will begin to relate to his spirit in a respectful fashion.

(P): Something happened when I did that. It's as if the spirit recognized me. That is really something. Can't believe that no one has ever talked about this. Except one of my grandmas once said something about this spirit stuff, but at the time I thought she was just talking old crazy stuff.

(T): Yes, this knowledge is older than dirt. All of our grandmas knew this. We've just forgotten the way. This brings us back to the "Good Red Road."

Transforming Suffering into Healing

The interventions described in this case are common in my day-to-day practice. Patients gain a sense of belonging and feel less powerless over the "White man's illness." It is critical for patients to have the insight that within our traditions we already have answers to situations in the present. I usually instruct patients to get their own "stash" of tobacco or cornmeal for their daily offerings. This practice consists of offering the tobacco or cornmeal to the spirit of alcohol in order to facilitate discussion and relationship with it. The relationship must be maintained daily; otherwise, the spirit of alcohol may begin to disrupt the patient's life due to the disrespect of being ignored. It is very bad manners to have had such a long relationship with this spirit and then to just try to discard it. This relation to the spirit of alcohol is in direct conflict with Western treatment in which the patient is not to have any contact with alcohol.

It is important to note that the offerings to the spirit of alcohol are done with awareness and intent. Basically, the relationship with alcohol also occurrs in A.A. models, except there the relationship is adversarial. Perhaps the adversarial relationship is in keeping with some of the societal norms, such as declaring war on everything from poverty to drugs. This type of psychology is not compatible with the psychology of Native People in which the restoration of harmony is of prime importance.

I tell patients that the drinking they have already done can provide insight in the future. If they continue to keep a spiritual relationship with alcohol, the alcohol will turn into its positive spiritual nature and provide them with insight about their lives. This is important because many patients feel guilt about the time that they have "wasted" while being in the crazy life-world of drinking. Allowing patients to find a way not to waste their suffering is important. I tell them to mindfully offer the suffering that they have already experienced to the well-being of other people who are suffering from addictions. Patients then can make existential use of their suffering and transform it into healing. *One of my favorite Sufi sayings in regarding this practice is, "Never be embittered by the amount of suffering that has been entrusted to you." This takes the metaphor to a new consciousness, and suffering can be understood as a means toward personal and collective transformation.*

Inpatient "Dreamtime Groups"

The use of dreams is another essential element to this healing method. Group therapy in a Western context usually consists of people sharing experiences and gaining insight by discussing these experiences with one another, while gaining further insight from the therapist. In this section, I will describe the use of dreamtime groups for inpatient settings. It is not the intent to give a course in dream interpretation here. Interested students may acquaint themselves with these methods in their graduate training and subsequent internships. Many inpatient settings provide only brief interventions, and patients usually are not able to go into the deeper causes of their problems, such as the soul wound and personal traumas. I have used dream groups in a twofold manner: first to deal with intrapsychic material emerging in a group context, and second to give patients a tool so that they can continue to work on their dreams when they leave treatment.

During the first meeting, there is usually some confusion because the patients are used to a structured group in which the facilitator tells them what is going on or what should be going on. When patients are allowed to be themselves and to explore their unconscious repressed material, they are suspicious and often revert to standardized 12-step or other comfortable group norms. Therefore, I give an introduction to dream work in a manner that makes at least intuitive sense to the folks in the group, along these lines:

Dreams are important to how we proceed on our healing journey. All of us dream. There is a reason for dreaming. As a matter of fact, this could be a dream dreaming itself right now. As human beings, we have lost the ability to communicate with the sacred because our egos have become so full of themselves. For this reason, Creator has invented a way in which she can go around our ego and still talk to us. Of course, for this to happen, we have to be asleep; otherwise, we would engage in denial, intellectualizing, and all sorts of defenses, because our egos want to believe that they are in control of the whole universe. Well, you can see where that has gotten all of you.

Ego is so tricky, though. If Creator were to talk to our unconscious in dreams using everyday language, guess what would happen? As soon as we wake up, we will start our defenses going and there goes the message out the window. Therefore, in Coyote fashion, Creator invented a tricky language that ego cannot understand and is full of symbols and images from the past, future, and whatnot. When we wake up and remember a dream, we usually have no idea what it's saying. Many of us just think of it as weird and don't pay attention to it. That's why we need to talk about the meaning of these weird images and try to decipher them. Once we see what's hidden in the symbols, our ego will have to move aside because the dreams don't mind insulting the ego.

When you have been under the influence of substances, this adds another layer to the problem of interpretation. The dream has to go through the fog of the alcohol and at times it's difficult to really see what the dream actually is conveying. That's why it's important that we take a look at your dreams now that you have some sobriety under your belts. Anyone had a dream?

At this point some of the group participants relate that they don't dream. This has to be validated, and the patients are told that perhaps they just don't remember. I tell them that it's like going into a dark cave. Once you shine your flashlight on certain objects, you can see them even though they have been there the whole time. Same thing happens with dreams. Once you start paying attention and shining the light of awareness on that part of the psyche, you may start seeing what's there.

Usually, there is a dreamer in the group who is willing to share a dream. At this point, I tell them that I will be writing the dream on a flip chart as accurately as I can. As the dreamer is relating the dream, I try to group the images as the dreamer tells them; that way, the group members can see how distinct one image is from another. Once the dream is written on the flip chart, I go to the first image and begin to ask the group for the in-terpretation of the image. This is repeated until the whole dream has been dealt with. We ask the dreamer if any of this makes sense, while giving the individual permission to not respond. At the end of the task, the sheet of paper is removed from the flip chart and I ceremoniously fold it and give it to the dreamer.

CASE #4:
INTERPRETING A DREAM WITHIN A GROUP SESSION

The dreamer in this case study is a woman in her 40s. She has been in several treatment programs. According to her, not much has helped to keep her in prolonged sobriety. There is always an underlying anxiety that eventually leads to relapse. The dream work depicted in this case is a small portion of the work that has to be accomplished by the group. In addition to the dream work, the group also will be working on underlying issues of historical trauma. The dialogue of the dream group is as follows:

Dreamer (D): I saw that I was in this house that I grew up in when I was 8 years old.

Interpretation (I): The group and I, along with the dreamer, felt that this image had to do with something that she needed to deal with that occurred around age 8. The dreamer is asked about what happened during that time of her life. This dreamer had severe trauma occurring during ages 7 through 10. This trauma results in a tremendous amount of material for the pa-tient to deal with in group and individual sessions.

(D): Then the scene changed and I was in the back of this pickup on this rough dirt road.

(I): The rough dirt road can be seen as how difficult her life has been recently. Her travel along life is bumpy and could become dangerous, as is the case with a patient that finds herself in re-covery.

(D): I noticed that no one was driving the pickup, and it appeared to be going out of control.

(I): No one is in charge. At least it appears as if no one is in charge. When asked about who actually may be driving the pickup, the dreamer and the group agree that it is the "spirit of alcohol." Therefore, the patient's life is out of control, and steps one and two of A.A. are critical for her.

(D): Finally, the pickup turned over and I could see that I was dying.

(I): Disaster is the only thing that can occur if the lifestyle doesn't change. Dying is a common image in dreams of patients that I have seen over the years. I tell them that this is a positive image. It is positive because their unconscious or spirit is giving them the transforming death/rebirth motif. In dying to their alcoholism, they will re-emerge as a new sober person. If they don't change their life, they very well may die a physical death; actually, the possibility of a physical death is pretty certain if they continue on this road.

(D): The dream then shifted to the first scene where I was at the old house again.

(I): The unconscious is taking the patient back to the first image. It is telling the patient that if she doesn't deal with the trauma that occurred during this time, the rest of the dream may come to pass. Therefore, the patient is confronted by her own spirit or unconscious, which makes this particularly strong image more acceptable than if the intervention came from an outside source such as a counselor.

By the time one dream has been deciphered, tremendous energy has been created in the group and there are many dreamers who come forth. At times, the group doesn't have enough time to deal with all the dreamers, and material has to wait until the next day. Patients will be encouraged to document their dreams and to try to interpret them utilizing the method outlined in the group. Dream groups have been one of the most profound treatment experiences that I have had and continue to have in my work. Patients appreciate getting in touch with an aspect of their lives that is vibrant and ongoing. They are surprised that no one has asked them about their dreams in the past and are extremely grateful to have this tool that can assist them in their life.

One of the greatest benefits of this method is that the psyche provides amazing relapse prevention through dreams. I have heard patients discuss dreams about situations and places that later materialized and had to do with relapse. By having advance warning of what is ahead, the patient can avoid the situation or else once in the situation recall the dream and the warning, which helps them to cope and perhaps avoid relapse.

CONCLUSION

In this chapter we have stepped into a different worldview in the attempt to understand addiction from an alternative perspective. It is interesting that within the Western paradigm there are those of like mind, such as Jung who also had an understanding that makes sense to Native People. The fact that Jung had such a deep sense of the entities involved in addiction is very encouraging. I believe that psychologically Natives and Euro-Americans have more similarities than we would think if we keep to a surface understanding. Cultural competence becomes more accessible as we travel the psyche, in which archetypes and other entities are free to roam and to form relationships with their human counterparts.

It is important to note that the soul-wounding process has left an emptiness in the soul of the wounded person. That emptiness of soul or spirit is seeking to fill the void with spirit. In our culture we see the quest for this fulfillment not only in craving substances, but also in other behaviors that become addictive, such as consumerism. Similarly, human beings from all walks of life seek fulfillment from various religious practices that are not necessarily spiritual and are distractions provided to us by our consumer culture as we become addicted to wanting and having more things. Therefore, we continue to exist in a meaningless existence where our soul becomes drained by the corporate vampire that is never satiated with the essence that he continuously sucks out of our being.

CHAPTER 6

Diagnosis: Treating Emotional
Problems as Living Entities

Padmasambava teaches: "From the eastern quarter of your brain
white Gauri (goddess) will appear to you, holding a corpse as a
club in her right hand and a skull-cup filled with blood in her left
hand. Do not be afraid" (Trungpa, 1975, p. 64).

IN THIS CHAPTER, the shifting of cultural metaphor will continue to
be clarified in actual clinical interventions. It may be somewhat more
difficult to make the shift when dealing with psychopathology (soul
suffering) that is not solely addictive in nature. When we go to the root
metaphor of any pathology, we find very simple and natural processes
that are manifested in different types of symptoms or behaviors. These
natural processes emerge from the psyche, and it bodes well to deal with
these processes in the most natural manner possible.

Over many years of working with Original People, I have found that
many suffer from what modern mental health systems diagnose as depression and other mood disorders. The labeling of the disorder in the
prescribed manner can leave the patient confused about what actually is
going to be dealt with in treatment. Thus, the treatment may not be as
useful as needed in order for the patient to be able to have a healthier and
happier life. This being the case, it is necessary at times to meet patients
in their world and work within their root metaphor to provide the best
treatment possible.

Even though I have dealt with addiction and emotional problems in
separate chapters, the problems usually occur simultaneously. More and
more, we find programs accommodating "dual diagnosis," and the separation between addictions therapists and mental health therapists is less-
ening to the point that soon the distinction will not be there. I believe that
this is a good trend that will decrease the fragmentation in our field that
has been transmitted to patients, who already come to us in a fragmented

state. How can we treat the patient fragmentation if we continue to be so compartmentalized and territorial in our own day-to-day experience as Healers? The answer is simple: We cannot.

In this chapter, I will discuss how I approach treatment of some of the problems that I have encountered over the years. There is no way that this will be an exhaustive examination of all the possible diagnostic categories. Again, I remind the reader that this approach is a healing process that can be used regardless of the diagnosis. This process deals with the problem or diagnosis as a living entity, not one that needs to be eliminated. I approach the problem as a living conscious being with which the patient needs to relate. If the Healer is centered and is not living in a paradigm in which the patient is seen as pathological, it will be a good starting point for the process. Also, bear in mind that the healing is an activity in which both Healer and patient are involved. Healing is an activity that can carry one through the process. It is not a system of subject and object, in which Healer and healed are at opposite ends of the spectrum.

Therapists interested in this approach also must be well trained in other approaches such as are available to all providers working in the Western context. I must reiterate that the seduction of wanting to "go Native" and immerse oneself in the world of spirits and the unconscious must be avoided. Patients who are seen in our clinics come from a life-world that is mostly Western, and they must be able to survive in that world. Therefore, the therapist must be able to utilize methods from that world to give the patient a well-rounded healing ceremony. In this ceremony, patients can discover for themselves the essence of who they are in relationship to that life-world and live in harmony in such a world. It is common for me to go from a behavioral intervention to one in which spiritual metaphor is being used and vice versa. Native people have a great flexibility as far as being able to step from the White into the Aboriginal world because this has been part of daily experience for the past 500 years.

VISITS BY DEPRESSION AND ANXIETY

As the title of this section indicates, we have already taken a detour from the conventional understanding of mood disorders, as they are known. The fact that these disorders are discussed as "visitors" removes the analysis from the sphere of Western psychology. Therapists must adjust their worldview to see that the identity of the patient is not dictated by a given diagnosis, as discussed in previous chapters. If we are going to name the problem, it is important to name it without making the problem an all-encompassing identity for the human being who presents with this type of soul suffering (psychopathology).

Most patients who are new to our world of treatment will describe their problem using phrases including "being sad," "being afraid," "feeling apprehension," "feeling something bad is about to happen," "if things go well, fearing that a terrible thing will follow," and so on. After getting to know the patient and hearing some of her dreams, it becomes possible to start working on the issue of depression or anxiety. Healers must always hold in mind the presence of historical trauma as they navigate the world of sadness or fear that the patient brings with her into her place of ceremony or office. Much of the sadness and fear is a reaction to trauma, in the same manner that we would find with a war veteran who recently has been diagnosed with posttraumatic stress disorder. The trauma that patients have to deal with is of a physical, emotional, and spiritual nature.

Family history is of great importance. Once the family history has been ascertained, it will facilitate the gathering of data to place the patient in the context of her tribal history. Once these pieces of the puzzle are in place, the Healer can start guiding the patient into the world of the soul wound and begin healing the soul wound. This type of therapy can move quickly if the patient and Healer are working from the same paradigm or worldview. If the patient is highly acculturated, the therapist needs to move more slowly to avoid alienating the patient, who also may be suffering from internalized oppression. In other words, the therapist cannot impose Traditional Native methods on a patient who may not value these methods due to the acculturation process.

Internalized oppression is expressed by patients as either an ignorance of culture or an aspiration to identify with mostly White middle-class consumer values. Patients who are suffering from internalized oppression need to move slowly through the paradigm described in this book. Otherwise, they will leave treatment. Patients who have been heavily Christianized may view the therapeutic approaches delineated in this book as "satanic" or "evil" because this is what they have internalized for generations. I do not mean to imply that being Christianized is itself a problem. The problem results when indoctrination of Christian people has been done in a manner that alienates Natives from themselves and causes suffering. I do not believe that Christ would have engaged in this type of oppressive behavior.

Not for Beginners

It is important to reiterate that these interventions are of an advanced nature simply because the therapist is expected to be well versed in both Western and Traditional Native practices. This requires a great amount of study, practice, and dedication that usually goes beyond the requirements of most graduate institutions. I caution the beginning therapist to be careful and to seek adequate supervision in attempting these liberation therapy practices. If appropriate supervision is not available by either a hybrid trained Western therapist or a Traditional Healer, *do not* attempt these interventions. I advise therapists to stay with their training and what is familiar. More will be said on supervision and some of the pitfalls in Chapter 8 on clinical supervision.

Due to the soul wounding that occurred over generations, many of the patients that present for help at clinics in Indian country are suffering with soul sadness or depression. During the time of the wounding process, our ancestors did not have the time to grieve or to heal from the ongoing wounding. The pain became repressed and regressed into the "black world" or the unconscious. Some of the anesthetizing behaviors used to cope with this pain were discussed in the previous chapter. Unresolved grief that has been passed on to the present generation is experienced as ongoing fear and sadness or, as our profession defines it, as anxiety and depression. The movement of grief from one generation to the next can be understood within the historical trauma paradigm described in the first two chapters of this book. Many patients express that there is a pain in their heart that will not go away, and the pain has been there as long as they can remember. There is also an ongoing sense of dread that things will continue to go badly and a pervasive sense of helplessness for many individuals, families, and communities.

Somatic Complications

The clinical picture is usually complicated by the fact that the patient is seeking to alleviate suffering by the use of alcohol or other substances. Many of our health systems do not address underlying issues of substance abuse, and the help given merely makes the patient dependent on medical interventions. Somatic problems, including chronic illnesses, are also very common and further complicate the clinical presentation.

Diabetes, hypertension, and respiratory and coronary illnesses are just some of the illnesses that flourish in our communities. These illnesses all have a high correlation with stress and the soul wound. Therefore, the Healer treating patients in Indian country must be cognizant that the suffering of the People is immense. At times, all of the possible interventions will appear to be of little or no use in the face of such huge problems. This is the time when Healers must understand that there is greater meaning in suffering and must not despair. Many Healers in Indian country burn out because they do not see immediate results. They may feel that they are powerless, and this may create a parallel process with the suffering that patients bring to them. Thus the problem becomes more hopeless. Therapists who are feeling hopeless because of the magnitude of the problems presented should seek out support from their peers and/or spiritual leaders. It is important to keep ourselves centered as we work to heal the soul wound. By keeping centered we should be safe from a possible soul wounding of our own.

CASE #5:
A PATIENT VISITED BY DEPRESSION AND ANXIETY

This patient is a female in her 40s who has been suffering from symptoms of major depression with episodes of anxiety. In addition, the patient has been dealing with medical problems brought on by many years of diabetes and resulting complications. The sessions are compressed in this study for the sake of continuity and brevity. As in the previous cases, it is assumed that the etiquette issues have been addressed. The patient has been asked whether she had been dreaming prior to beginning therapy. She has received medical attention as well as ongoing Western problem-solving, supportive, cognitive-behavioral, as well as insight therapy.

She has tried to self-medicate with alcohol but stopped due to fear of death because of health complications of diabetes. The patient is living in an urban area, as are most Native people in this country, and is subjected to daily episodes of racism and disenfranchisement. She believes in Traditional Native religion but does not have an ongoing spiritual practice that gives her life meaning. She reports that she does dream but usually does not remember her dreams. She is not sure why she is being asked about this in the first place. She also has a history of sexual abuse, but she has little recollection of the trauma. She has never dealt with the abuse because she is fearful of being overwhelmed. Her previous alcohol abuse, which provided a boundary against intrusive painful thoughts, was an unconscious attempt at self-medication.

The Initial Sessions

The following dialogue occurred over the course of seven therapy sessions. The sessions also contained Western therapeutic interventions, which will not be discussed here because the purpose in this book is to introduce another form of therapy and not to revisit existing ones.

(T): I see that you've been suffering for some time with sadness and fear. Also, no dreams, eh? Keep an eye out for dreams.

(P): Dreams? What can that do? I came for help. I have a major depression. (*The patient has bought into the pathological model and is identifying with the illness as she perceives it.*)

(T): Major depression? Who told you that?

I'm starting to deconstruct the pathological model that the patient has internalized. By asking who diagnosed her, I am beginning the process of explaining the naming ceremony that is in the diagnostic process.

(P): All of the therapists I've had so far. About four of them. Also, my medical doctor says I have it.

(T): What is that? I mean major depression?

This is a stupid Columbo-type question that will get the patient to think about how she attained this belief system. It serves also as assessment of acculturation.

(P): Are you kidding? I thought you were a psychologist. You know what major depression is. At least, I hope you do.

(T): I know how it's defined. I also know that the definition changes with time. Right now the definition is from this book. (*I hold the DSM-IV so that she can see it. I turn to the page where major depression is described. I let the patient see the criteria for the diagnosis. This serves to demystify the diagnostic process and to empower her.*) Do you have some of the symptoms listed here?

(P): Yeah. I sure do. Looks like I have it.

(T): According to this, it sure looks like it. We have to find a way to move it on. That's why you're here, aren't you?

I use this language of "moving it on" in order to be able to start the discussion of the "spirit of depression." By my changing the way that the depression is discussed, the patient may realize that there is another way of dealing with the situation. This also gets the patient's interest. By talking about "moving it on," the depression is discussed as something objective that doesn't belong to the patient and can be moved into another place.

(P): Move it on? What is that? I never heard anyone say it like that.

(T): Some of our traditions believe that most illnesses, emotions, and such have a spirit to them. Somehow, our spirit attracts these energies when there are things in our life that aren't in harmony. Sometimes, these visitors come to visit from the past. You could say that these visitors actually visited our ancestors and at times they are passed on down to us. If we don't deal with them now, our kids and grandkids on down will have to deal with them. (*This is an important insight for the patient. It can lead to the discussion of intergenerational trauma.*) You know, everything we do will impact seven generations. Not only seven generations to come, but also seven generations in the past.

(P): Never heard it like that. Past generations?

(T): Yes. When our ancestors were genocided, they did not get the opportunity to grieve or to heal. Sometimes, we have to do that for them.

(P): That's a new idea. Never heard of such a thing.

(T): I'm not saying that all of your sadness, I mean depression, is caused by the sadness of your ancestors. There may be things in your personal life causing it and we will look at all of these. It's a more complete "look see." After all, you had therapy before and you're still sad. Can't hurt to try to look in other places.

(P): Makes sense. So far, not much has worked. I take all these medications, and they just make me numb. Somehow, I'm still depressed and sad. Afraid of being really depressed. That's an awful feeling.

(T): Fear is also something that can be passed on down from our ancestors. Imagine how afraid they were when all that craziness of all the killing was going on? They never got the chance to even tell anyone they were afraid, because there would be yet another disaster that would happen even before the smoke cleared.

This is giving her historical trauma 101 information. This serves to bring the historical context into the therapy as well as to help her objectify the problem. It is important that she begin to realize that she is not defective. Instead, she is reacting to a situation in the same fashion that most people would.

(P): Must have been really something. This is really sad to think about. How can it be affecting me, if I never knew this stuff?

(T): How it happens is not completely known yet. I think that the spirit of sadness attached itself to our ancestors, and no one has attempted to heal this energy. Then there's your own personal stuff that attracts this energy, and no wonder you're so sad. The sadness attracts the spirit of fear because you become afraid that the depression will get really bad and that it will never end. Right?

(P): Well yah. It doesn't end. It does get really bad at times, and I would do anything to stop this.

(T): Anything? Like what?

(P): Sometimes, I feel like if I wasn't here it would stop.

(T): You mean like if you died? Have you thought about killing yourself?

(P): Well, sure. I mean, who wants to go on like this? This is so tiring.

(T): So far, though, you've decided to be here. I mean you haven't killed yourself. And as far as I know, you've tried only once but you called for help.

(P): At the last minute, I wondered if it was the right thing to do. You know. I didn't want to fry in hell forever.

(T): Now that would be depressing. Forever? Frying forever, yah, that would be very depressing. You're not going to try again, are you?

(P): No, I'm not thinking like that. I mean, I wish I was dead, but I don't want to be the one to do it. Hey, wait. I did have a dream. In the dream, I saw myself laying there and I was dead. Can't believe that I just remembered that so clearly.

(T): That's a good dream.

This is confusing for patients. Confusion will allow them to be less resistant for the time being. Confusion techniques are common in Aboriginal Healing and are used to bring balance. If the patient is too serious, humor is used. If the patient is not serious, then serious talk or metaphor is employed to restore balance.

(P): What? What do you mean a good dream?

(T): Well, death usually means the end of something. In your dream, it could mean the end of you as a sad person. It doesn't have to be the end of you as a person. Perhaps, it is showing you that the visitor called sadness or depression may be moving on, or transforming into something else. This is what happens when there is a death, you know. There is a complete transformation. So when you say that you want to die, I see that as a good thing. You're telling me that your old self needs a death–rebirth experience.

(P): Never thought of it like this. This is really different, the way you talk. Are you like a real psychologist? I mean no one ever said this stuff to me. Interesting, very interesting. This is making too much sense. I mean the idea of my ancestors, that is really interesting. All this spirit stuff. This is how my grandma talked. I remember her talking about things like this. I thought they were just stories. You make it sound real, like it's right now.

(T): Grandmas know a lot. If it sounds real, it's because your spirit is resonating with the spirit of the words. Words have power, you know? Whatever you put out into the air has a lot of power, and it goes all over the world.

(P): I've heard that too. Somehow, this sadness, or depression, or whatever is starting to look different.

(T): Like how different?

(P): It seems as if it's not really me. I mean it bothers me, and I suffer, but it looks different than it did.

The patient is beginning to gain objectivity over her problem. She is no longer the problem. Instead, there is a problem that is present and visiting, which makes it more workable than if she is the problem. If she is the problem, the only way to get rid of the problem is to get rid of herself, which can lead to suicidal acting out. The patient is moving out of the pathology paradigm and into a relationship one that is more in tune with her culture.

The above conversations took seven sessions. During those sessions, our work also included problem solving of daily life issues such as economic and other social needs. The patient worked with a case manager to obtain some of the necessities that were missing in her life, such as adequate living conditions, nourishing food, and attending social events. These strategies must be balanced with the patient's physical and spiritual needs in order for the interventions to have optimum use to the patient. It would serve no purpose to simply have patients pray and not give them a piece of bread for their sustenance.

The Next Ten Sessions

In the following sessions, we began to deal with the deeper personal and historical issues that fueled the patient's depression and anxiety. Dreaming was becoming more common, and the patient became very interested in the process. Sometimes symptoms decreased, then increased. When symptoms increased, the patient utilized the skills of observation she had developed through understanding the metaphor discussed and cognitive behavioral strategies. Behavioral strategies involved her use of journaling, paying attention to behavioral antecedents and consequences. These strategies worked well to increase objectivity by enhancing mindfulness.

This particular patient was an introverted/feeling type. The strategies helped her to develop her thinking function. Through the development of a more extraverted/thinking ability, she gained objectivity, helping her to see her situation more clearly and without as much attachment. Lack of attachment increased her ability to avoid engaging with fear. This, in turn, helped reduce the depression and the cycle slowed down considerably.

In the next 10 sessions, we began to explore the sexual trauma and the impact of the abuse on her sadness and fear. Some of her physical problems were also associated with the sexual trauma that she suffered.

During this treatment phase, the patient was attending sessions regularly and had hope that her life would improve. She started taking computer skills classes to improve her standard of living. Her ego strength had increased so that the trauma could be addressed without fear of overwhelming her. Of course, this had to be done with care and with permission from the unconscious. In my work, I address issues of this nature only after dreams have given permission to venture into the place of trauma. In working with traumatized people over the years, I have found that the unconscious material in dreams is the best guide as to where the treatment needs to progress. Otherwise, we run the risk that the patient will experience a psychotic break, or some other form of splitting/dissociating that will greatly complicate the individual's life and may halt treatment.

The patient began this phase of treatment with a series of dreams in which she was being chased by a dark figure. These dreams allowed an opening for treatment of the sexual trauma and understanding of the legacy of historical trauma on the current high incidence of sexual abuse in Indian country.

(P): I had several dreams in which a shadowy or dark person was chasing me. It was very scary. I don't know who it was or what its face looked like.

(T): How close was it getting to you?

I ask this in order to know how close we are to starting discussion of the issues of the abuse. In Jungian terms, this shadowy figure could be an archetypal image that is trying to get the attention of the ego so the ego can begin to explore this aspect of the patient's life. Another possibility is that this negative image is a hostile animus figure. Animus *is the term Jung used to describe the masculine side of a female's psyche. There are parallels in Aboriginal cultures that describe the essence of animus in a manner that is readily understood by the patient. I usually talk about the divinities, represented in sand paintings and other art forms that always include a balance of light and dark, male and female, and other contrasting energies that exist in the field of the present reality. I explain to the patient that the masculine representation is an aspect of her soul or spirit, and of course the female represented in the dream would be the opposite, or anima, as Jung termed it. Once this understanding has been given, the patient can begin to understand how she has internalized a negative or hostile aspect of the masculine energy that was used to cause the trauma or injury in the first place. Most patients, regardless of educational background, readily understand these important theoretical constructs because most of these metaphors are used in ceremonial forms that the patient has either participated in or heard of from others.*

(P): It was getting pretty close. It was like I could feel its breath on me.

(T): Is there any way that you could turn around in the dream and see who this is?

(P): I don't think so. I'm running and it's too scary. It's out of my control. (*The fact that it's out of the patient's control may be indicative of the situation that is being depicted by this figure, namely, the abuse in which the victim has no control.*)

(T): What do you think it might look like if you did get to see it?

This is an attempt to begin a process of active imagination in which the ego can have some control of the image by working through imagination. The patient must be cautioned not to attempt this type of exercise outside of the office. The container must be preserved until the healing has gained some awareness of its own. I tell patients that just as the illness is an entity, so is healing. This concept is consistent with Native beliefs. The spirit of healing is an important entity to have in the process, and it must be respected and acknowledged in common with all of the other entities. Making offerings to the healing spirits is part of the process that the therapist as well as the patient need to engage in as part of the manners that are required when dealing in the therapeutic or healing circle.

(P): If I could see it, well, not that I want to, it probably looks like some sort of vampire or something like that. Not that I have ever seen a vampire, but like in the movies you know.

(T): Vampire . . . hmmmm. These creatures have curious ways about them. Do you know anything about these fellows?

I am making the connection to the mythology of vampires, which closely parallels the process of the sexually abused person in relationship with the perpetrator. This can help provide insight into the difficulty of dealing with the abuse. This phase must be done with great care and observation of patient's affect. If the patient starts to get upset, it's important to back off and either leave it for another day or perhaps create a spiritual container with smoke. I prefer sage smoke at this time because sage is known for its purifying properties and a lot of folks believe that sage actually can chase evil forces away. Readers may refer to Chapter 2 for some vampire mythology that can be used at this point.

(P): No, not much. I just know that you can't kill them in a regular way. It takes a special stick or a silver bullet to do this. Something that's been blessed by a priest or someone like that. You know, like a Mr. Pointy.

(T): What? Mr. who?

(P): Mr. Pointy like in Buffy the Vampire Slayer. (*The patient is referring to a T.V. show that has been very popular for several years.*

In the show the heroine, Buffy, walks around at night finding and slaying vampires. This is an interesting complex that has emerged recently in the American psyche.)

(T): So it sounds like it will take special medicine to deal with this shadowy figure in the dream then? Sometimes these figures in dreams can represent an aspect of our own spirit. Since you're a female, this could be speaking to a part of your male spirit.

(P): It sure will. Yeah, I think it would take something powerful to deal with him. This guy is pretty gnarly. What do you mean by male spirit?

(T): Yes. In the teachings of our old ones, they talk about how we're half male and half female. Your soul happens to be male and mine female. You see, you're half of your father and half of your mother. I mean that's biology; you don't have to see it any other way if you don't want to. When you get hurt by a male energy, that male energy distorts your masculine spirit. Sometimes that energy from the vampire sits in there creating problems for you. Just because you're not aware of it, doesn't mean it's not there. Okay, so let's offer some prayer smoke and create a circle here for you. That way, you're protected from this vampire or whatever it is. In a way, the dream is bringing you a gift. It may be a scary one, but it's a gift because it's letting you explore and gain insight. So, you should give a gift to the dreamtime.

Over the years, I have asked patients to give a gift of food, water, tobacco, cornmeal, or whatever they wish to the dream. Aboriginal thought teaches that in order to complete the relationship in a healing circle, one must give a gift to the spirit of the medicine that is deeply involved in the process. In this manner, patients continue to deepen their relationship to their own process outside of the therapeutic office or healing circle. The process of termination is much easier if the Healer is more of a "prop" rather than the one in charge of the process. Transference issues also can be diverted away from the Healer toward the process itself. Of course, this may be deflating to the ego of the therapist/Healer. However, it also will protect the Healer because the Healer also can project their countertransference onto the healing process. It is important that therapists realize that they are merely a vessel through which the healing process flows rather than the one in control.

(P): Never thought about it like that. This is amazing stuff, and it makes more sense all the time. It's weird, but it makes sense. Oh, thanks. *(At this point I present the burning sage close to the patient.*

The patient draws smoke toward herself with both hands in a ceremonial fashion. When she's done, I draw some to myself to complete the protection of the healing container that we are both in at that moment.)

(T): It's always good to have some prayer smoke. Not just in these situations but most of the time. One can never be blessed too much, you know? By the way, do you have some sage at home? (*Amazingly, many of the people I have worked with do not. This presents an opportunity to give them sage, which also can act as a transitional object. In this way the therapy session goes with them and provides containment for them.*)

(P): No, I haven't had any in a while.

(T): What kind of Indian are you anyway?

I say this with some laughter in order to bring balance into the session with humor. After all, we need to balance out the vampire image with some lightheartedness. This provides the patient a moment without stress and helps her to see that she also can utilize humor in her life situation and not have to be in sadness all the time. Non-Native therapists will have to come up with some other type of humor at this point, unless they have such a strong relationship with the patient that will allow this particular form of humor. Otherwise, the patient may see this remark as a racial slur.

(P): Well, a good Indian (laughs).

(T): (*I ceremoniously take some sage from a drawer and wrap it in a tissue. I reach over and hand this to the patient. The patient takes it in a somber and ceremonious manner and puts it in her purse.*) There you go. Now its purpose is to be used, okay? Don't just leave it wrapped up. There's plenty of sage in the world, so don't be stingy with it.

Non-Native Healers can do this once they have internalized some of these beliefs into their own lives. I have seen several doctoral interns who are "White" do very well with this type of intervention, but it has to be genuine. If non-Native Healers have not internalized Aboriginal spiritual form, they can use the form that they resonate with to create the spiritual boundary. Healers who do not have a spiritual practice should just stay with what they know and refer the patient for the spiritual interventions.

(P): Yes, I'll use it. I'll smoke off my place as soon as I get there. Thanks, this is good.

(T): You know, that vampire could be the spirit of incest. Like we've been talking about for some time. Everything has a spirit and awareness. The same goes for something like incest. This

is pretty weird, eh? But we have to be consistent. All these energies have a purpose. Some of them are not pleasant and are
downright painful, but they all have a teaching and medicine
right in them. So, we shouldn't be afraid of them once we understand this. Of course, before we understand, they are very
frightening and that's normal. . . . I mean to be frightened at
that time.

*The issue of incest was already known to me since she had been in
therapy before. Otherwise, the topic would have been introduced more
delicately. I would have allowed her to bring it up through the process of
exploring the dream. I would have alluded to the notion of the vampire
and what it could mean, if this had not been part of her history that we
were both aware of.*

(P): What?

(T): I think you heard me. It's probably the spirit of incest that
has been chasing you for a long time. You know that anything
that interferes with life has a spirit. It has to be alive in order to
mess with your life in the first place. If it was a dead or inani-
mate thing, it probably wouldn't bother you. The fear and sadness could be part of that. Also, some of your physical sickness
could be part of what that energy is doing to you.

*This may sound bizarre to the Western psyche. Spirit of incest is a notion
that gets the attention of the patient in a truly remarkable manner. The
archaic image that this creates is much more energized than just saying,
"sexual trauma," which is fairly neutral in comparison. In order to deal
with these hostile forces in the psyche, we must know who they are and
name them. After all, we don't have problems in naming our patients
with the DSM-IV, which falls short of giving the patient the most appropriate image of the energy that is creating intense pain in her life.
Why should we get apprehensive in naming the forces that are killing our
patients?*

(P): This is getting a little scary.

(T): Well, let's slow it down. I can explain what I mean.

(P): Sure.

(T): You see, when someone is hurt that way, it's a big violation.
Especially when it's done to a child, because a child is sacred.
The injury is to the body, mind, and spirit. With me?

(P): Yeah. So the whole person is violated?

(T): Yes. The body knows how to heal itself and does so fairly
quickly, but it still remembers. The mind protects itself by for-

getting. The spirit gets infected by the spirit of the vampire. You know, like in the movies. Once a vampire bites you, you know what happens?

(P): Then you become a vampire.

(T): Unless someone with powerful medicine can intervene.

(P): So then, I don't have to become a vampire?

(T): No. When the perpetrator abuses you, some of the perpetrator's spirit is also shot into you. Like in witchcraft or sorcery. Perpetrators are sorcerers, you know. Someone did sorcery on them, and then they became sorcerers because no one helped to heal them.

In this sorcery discussion, I also am setting up the discussion of historical trauma by using stupid Columbo-type questions. It is important to start making the connections between historical trauma and the level of incest present in our communities. I am not trying to paint a picture of a "noble savage" who was enlightened before the White man came. Of course, there were human problems. The human problems were greatly magnified by the soul wounding caused by colonization of the People of Turtle Island. Of course, the sorcery that was brought over from Europe had its roots in the soul wounding that had occurred to our White relatives over the millennia in Europe, where they were also both victims and perpetrators of genocide. The internalized violence of many generations then was brought to Turtle Island, and that energy spread through the souls of the people like a forest fire that is out of control. Wounding was seeking to wound itself. At the same time, the wounding spirit recognized the healing energy that was part of the Earth itself on Turtle Island because the Earth had not been as wounded here on Turtle Island as it had been in Europe after so many generations of violence.

(P): Sorcery? No wonder this goes so deep and is so hard to heal from. This will take medicine of a special kind.

(T): Yes. Medicine of a special kind, that is already within you. Where do you think the sorcery came from?

(P): Well, my stepdad was the one that hurt me.

(T): Where did he get his sorcery from?

(P): I have heard stories that his uncle abused him when he was little.

(T): I wonder what happened to the uncle to turn him into a vampire?

(P): Guess someone hurt him.

(T): So, is this part of your tradition? Seems like a lot of people did this in your family.

This is almost an insulting question and the answer is obvious. The intent is to get her to think in a historical manner and trace the origins of the incest problem in her family and community. Some patients have done such a thorough research job that they can pinpoint the time, place, and people responsible for bringing the abuse to their community.

(P): No, it's not part of my tradition.

(T): Wonder who the first vampire was?

(P): First vampire?

(T): There had to be a beginning to all this, right?

(P): Yeah, I guess so. Everything has a beginning, as they say.

(T): Any of your ancestors forced to go to boarding school?

(P): Yes. I've heard stories of how my grandparents were herded like cattle and put on trains not knowing where they were going.

Patient becomes pensive, and it is obvious that she is connecting historical events, which are well known in Indian country. Many of the boarding schools were havens for vampires who abused Native children physically, sexually, and spiritually.

(T): Did your family talk about what happened to your grandparents after they were sent away?

(P): They, I mean we weren't allowed to pray, or speak our language, or dress in our way, or to be Indian in any way.

(T): There was also a lot of sexual abuse of the children. It's well documented now, you know. The schoolmasters, priests, and whoever physically and sexually abused the kids.

(P): So, the first vampires in our community were from the boarding schools. That's where all this started. And we think that we're just a bunch of crazy Indians. This isn't right. I can't believe that they are the vampires and we're the ones feeling guilty all this time.

(T): That's what vampires do. When they shoot their sorcery into the victim, they also shoot their shame and guilt into the person they are abusing. Then the victim feels like it's her fault. Bet you have felt some guilt about all this over the years?

(P): A lot of guilt. I thought there was something wrong with me. If there wasn't something wrong with me, then this wouldn't have happened. I've felt really ashamed.

(T): The guilt and shame also can cause all kinds of sickness. When one feels guilty, there's usually only one way to undo the guilt. If you're feeling guilty, it's usually because you've done something wrong. The only way to undo this is through some sort of sacrifice, kinda like a scapegoat. You know about scapegoats?

(P): Yeah. Something about the sins of the community were placed on the goat. Then the goat was sacrificed. Poor goat, wasn't the goat's fault.

(T): Exactly. No fault on the goat's part, but the goat still has to shed blood in order to balance out the sins of the community.

(P): That's pretty heavy. This is interesting and weird at the same time.

(T): Wonder how you're playing the scapegoat part in your life?

(P): (*After extended silence*) . . . whew, I have. But I've still felt so much guilt.

(T): With all that guilt, you must be giving or you've given some sort of blood sacrifice in order to bring balance. You're probably unconscious of the blood sacrifice you have given.

(P): Sure am.

(T): Your medical chart shows you've had several surgeries in your life. Also, diabetes is causing you a lot of suffering. You've been overweight. Looks to me like you've been sacrificing your body to the guilt and shame.

I take the burning bowl with cedar in it and burn some. I explain to the patient that cedar is a blessing. A short explanation is that cedar is there to catch the first ray of sun every morning even if we are not. When we burn the cedar, we release the blessing of a thousand sunrises that are given to us in this very moment. Usually patients feel that this will offer protection and blessing on their healing path, regardless of the forces that are acting against them.

Another Descent into Sadness

At this point in the treatment, the patient became very depressed. This is an indication that we're approaching very disturbing material or we are getting close to the "vampire complex." I slowed down the process and directed attention to the sadness or depression. In the next few sessions, I encouraged the patient to relate to the sadness much in the same way that patients deal with the spirit of alcohol. Again, these are different means of seeing the world that may seem "weird," but to the Native patient suffering from these problems, it is more "weird" to just talk about diagnoses and cognitions. Therefore, focus is given to the actual sadness or spirit of depression and anxiety, because these two entities seem to travel together.

(P): I've been so sad during the past few days. A deep sadness and
    fear too.
(T): Do you know where you feel it? I mean in your body?
(P): Right in here (*pointing to an area under her heart*).
(T): Your heart seems to be trying to want to tell you something.
(P): There you go again. You have to go into these kind of places.
(T): I believe that we experience pain of all sorts to make us pay at-
    tention. If everything is going good, then we don't stop to even
    offer a little prayer, you know?
(P): Guess you're right. What could it be trying to tell me?
(T): Any dreams? You know that's usually how "spirit" informa-
    tion of this type comes through.
(P): No, not really. Still I'm wondering about all that vampire stuff.
(T): Tell you what. Have you ever heard of the "I' Ching"?
(P): No, what's that? Itching?
(T): It's I' Ching. It's probably the oldest book in the world. It's a
    kind of oracle that can help us find out the meaning of a situa-
    tion in a point in time.

*I have been using the I' Ching in my work for years. I find that it helps
validate the process when patients are not feeling as if they are progress-
ing. Every time that I have used the oracle, the patient is very surprised
at the directness and relevance of the hexagram that they acquire.*

*For those who are completely unaware of the I' Ching, whole I' Ching
kits are available for purchase at any bookstore. When the I' Ching is used
in therapy, the patient is asked to throw three coins, six times. By a systematic addition of the three coins, a "line" is derived after each toss of the
coins. The line can be either a yin (open) line or yang (solid) line. When
six lines are derived, then a hexagram is obtained. These lines can corre-
spond only to one of the 64 hexagrams in the I' Ching or book of changes.
Once the hexagram is obtained, the appropriate hexagram is consulted in
the book of changes and the appropriate consult from the oracle is given to
the patient.*

(P): Sounds interesting. Can it help?
(T): Yah. Want to try one?
(P): Sure, can't hurt.
(T): Okay. Here's three coins. Throw them six times. Then we'll
    look up the specific advice for you in this situation. (*Patient
    throws the coins very mindfully as I write down the corresponding
    lines.*)
(P): There. Now what?
(T): Let's see. You got this one. The most specific advice is in line

six. It says: "A goat butts against a hedge. It cannot go backward, it cannot go forward. Nothing serves to further. If one notes the difficulty, this brings good fortune" (Baynes, 1950). Well, what do you think?

(P): Sounds like that's where I'm at. I'm kinda stuck.

(T): That's what I think. It's also telling you that if you become aware of this, then you will be brought good fortune.

(P): I noticed that. What does that mean? How do I do that? I mean note the difficulty? (*Patient smiles as she asks. She has some hope that things will change and the oracle is reinforcing this.*)

(T): That's what we're doing right now. We're paying attention to the difficulty. Just by bringing this into awareness, you've already changed the quality of the depression. You see, once you see or make contact with a spirit, it changes the relationship. Instead of the spirit just bugging you on its own trying to get your attention, you're responding just like when someone calls your name and you answer. As soon as you answer, the process changes.

(P): Interesting. Makes sense. Then what?

(T): This is going to sound pretty weird. Guess you should be used to that by now, since you've been coming here for a while.

(P): Not anymore. Actually, I expect it. It wouldn't be interesting if we were just talking about the same old psychobabble (laughs).

(T): Sounds like you're becoming a "born again pagan," eh?

We both laugh. Again, humor is critical when working with someone who is so sad. The patients need to experience a shift in affect so that they can begin to understand that the sadness is not permanent and can shift given the right conditions. If we allow patients to stay depressed the whole time, we are doing them a great disservice. Therefore, I suggest that all Healers/therapists acquire a repertoire of jokes and humor that can be used at the right time. I must caution that timing is critical.

(P): Well? What is it? What's this new weird thing? (*Patient is interested and curious, which is always a good sign. I interpret this as receptivity for the new insight that is ready to emerge.*)

(T): You asked. What you need to do next is to bless the sadness.

(P): What?

(T): You heard me. Bless the sadness.

(P): Now that makes no sense. I don't want the sadness. Blessed or not.

(T): That's the whole thing right there (*I don't use the word problem, but instead use "thing" to avoid pathologizing*). You're struggling

with the sadness. The more you struggle, the more energy
you use. And guess what? The more energy you use, the more
energy the sadness gets. And when that happens, guess what
happens?

(P): I get more depressed?

(T): Exactly. Well done. See you know weird stuff too! (*We both
laugh.*)

(P): So when I bless it what happens?

(T): Well, think on it. Study on this. (*Silence for a while.*)

(P): There's no struggle. There's kind of a separation of some sort.

(T): Hey, why do you even need me to talk to? You know this stuff.
(*At this point, I'm validating the patient's ability to make insights.
I'm also letting her know that I'm just a "prop" that will facilitate the
termination process when the time comes.*)

(P): Well, not so fast. I still need to come here.

(T): Yes, for now. But in time, you'll know how to do this for yourself.

(P): How do I bless it?

(T): Same way you bless yourself. You have to be very soft with
it. You see, the spirit of the sadness is also very shy, like a little
baby. You want to move very softly toward it and bless it very
softly so that you can start to relate to it.

*I light some sweet-grass and move the smoking braid toward the patient.
I model the soft movements of blessing in a style that is slow as in Tai
Chi movement. The patient proceeds to bless the sadness in her heart in
the same manner. I can see an almost trancelike concentration in her face.
When she is done, she smiles.*

(P): Wow. Something happened there.

(T): Yes, the spirit of the sadness recognized you, and you recognized it for the first time. Now, you can begin to have conversations with it since you've shown that your grandma taught
you manners. See, it's so rude not to approach spirit beings in
a way that shows good manners. Usually, we just want them
to go away. Gosh, what would your relatives say if you just
"shooed" them off every time they came to visit? They would
think that pretty rude and probably would start gossiping and
thinking badly of you, eh?

(P): So simple. This is so simple. How come no one talks about this
stuff? I actually can have a relationship with this spirit now.
Wonder what it will say?

*She is interested in understanding the underlying message or insight of
the depression. It is no longer a simple pathology to be gotten rid of. She*

has entered an existential reality that will give her meaning and hope in a manner in which she has never really had. The success in this instant strengthens her faith in the process. The therapeutic alliance is strong and the patient is trusting these "weird" interventions and actually looking forward to them. This will set up the treatment for the sexual abuse, which will be approached in a similar manner.

The Spirit of Suicide

Interventions such as this are also appropriate when the patient is visited by the spirit of suicide or has suicidal ideation. I ask the patient to make an offering to the spirit of suicide, which I introduce early on as the "spirit of transformation." I tell the patient that the idea of wanting to die is literally a misinterpretation of the soul's desire to transform.

Unfortunately, the ego interprets transformation as a physical death, which really serves no purpose in the soul's quest for fulfillment. I tell patients, "You cannot 'unkill' yourself," and that therefore power and control are completely lost if they decide to take that avenue. I tell them if they realize they made a mistake after they have killed themselves, that would be even more depressing and who knows how long this would last. Once patients grasp the meaning of the "suicide image," they gain interest in what the spirit of suicide may have in store for them in the future.

During the session, I ask patients who are exhibiting suicidal ideation to have a conversation with the spirit of suicide. The patients approach the conversation with all the mannerisms expected in a polite exchange and ask the suicide spirit what it wants from them. I then ask patients to leave an offering for the spirit of suicide as an expression of gratitude for the gift that this entity has brought. In the manner stated in the above scenario, I ask them to bless the suicide spirit, which completely changes the relationship with this energy. Of course, the usual Western interventions, such as suicide contract and hospitalization, also are used to best intervene in this most serious event in a patient's life. This approach also will empower patients in future times when the spirit of suicide may return. The patients will continue to have existential meaning in their life instead of being ongoing victims as is often the case in lives that are plagued by depression. The patients realize that suicidal images have a transforming energy that literally can take them into the depths of their psyche, which has been suffering from personal and intergenerational grief.

(T): Now that you have met the suicide spirit, what do you think? Is it what you thought?

(P): Not at all. Now it makes sense. The dream with the vampire.

Trying to kill me. It's okay if I let him kill me. Kill that part that needs to die.

(T): Dying. What could that mean? (*Here's a Columbo-type question that will assist her in gaining insight into the death/rebirth motif.*)

(P): Well, everything dies. It's just the way things are.

(T): Yes, and it all has a purpose of some kind. Like when you plant a seed of corn in the ground. You bury it, huh?

Guiding the discussion to a resurrection image. It is critical that the patient realize that the death process is part of a larger ongoing process of transformation. The corn idea assists in this insight. Corn is regarded as a very sacred plant and integral to the life process, which includes death.

(P): The corn seed dies in the Earth. Then, it comes up again. Is that what I'm trying to do? Never thought of it that way. So, when I wanted to kill myself, I really wanted to live? Live in another way? Hmmm . . . (*silence for about 1 minute*). Yes, the suicide spirit actually was trying to help me. How come no one ever said anything about this?

(T): You're very insightful. The suicide spirit is trying to show you something. That's why I asked you to leave it an offering. Remember manners? All spirits are good. They are here to help us. It's just that our egos like to control the universe. Last time I checked, Creator was still in charge of the universe (laughter). It's best when we don't fight against these energies. Take it from me, I've never won a single one of these fights, so it's like Creator 10,000 and me zero. You would think I'd get a clue and stop the struggle, eh?

Here I'm letting the patient know that we all struggle and get attached to our egos. In doing so, the transference is lessened and she can belong to the same human family that the Healer is part of. This minimizes the distance between us and yet maintains the sacred healing boundary. Many therapists who have been trained in psychodynamic models that have their foundations in psychoanalysis, would have problems with this type of disclosure. In most Traditional societies, the Healer lives among the community so there are no secrets. This is a reality today in the Native community, which is very small, and word travels via the "moccasin telegraph" all over the hemisphere with incredibly rapid efficiency. This was the case even before the Internet. Therefore, Healers/therapists working in Indian country really have to live their lives in a manner that will stand up to this scrutiny and is consistent with the well-being that they are requesting of their patients.

(P): When you put it that way, it really makes me wonder why we fight so much against all this. I know it's part of our way to live more naturally and flow with things. I guess we've learned a lot of bad habits over the generations. A lot has been lost.

(T): I hear a lot of people say that. I mean that a lot has been lost. Where do you think it got lost? Where is it?

Over the years, a lot of patients have expressed this sense of loss of culture. My purpose here is to guide the patient to realizing that the essence of the cultural "ways" are still here on the very Earth that gave them birth in the first place. Also, the insight that the ways are not static but are fluid and alive is important. The ways need to be fresh and new if they are to be viable in our present-day life-world. Of course, access to the Earth's consciousness emerges through our earth body, which can act as a translator for earth consciousness through the dreamtime and the dreams that dream the patient.

(P): You mean the ways?

(T): Yes, the ways.

(P): Never really thought about it. Guess they're around for those that know how to find them.

(T): How do you think the ways came in the first place?

(P): Guess Creator gave visions and such to special people. Then they brought the vision to the people.

(T): So, it sounds like there was a day when the first ceremony of a certain type was held? Wonder why they did the particular ceremony on that very day?

(P): There must have been a need for the prayer.

(T): Exactly. There was a need that the ceremony fulfilled. Just like there is a need today for certain types of prayers and healing.

(P): Wow. I thought that tradition was all set. Sounds like you're talking about changing it. Makes sense. The world is different. We do need new "ways" and new prayers. This is really interesting. It gives a whole new way to seeing things. We're not just stuck with what we're told. We have to come up with new ideas. Be creative. I like this (smiling).

(T): Guess you've been doing some of that in your own life, eh?

(P): You mean like the therapy?

(T): Kinda. Must admit you've said that this is different from any other kind of therapy or ceremony you've been to. And it has all come from you. You have invented your own ceremony. I have a lot of admiration for you.

(P): Thanks. Makes me feel like I haven't wasted my life. Like I'm part of something bigger.

At this point, the patient's ego is strong and will be able to sustain the final phase of the treatment, which will be to deal with the sexual abuse. We have already seen the vampire appear, which signals that this is a vital area. In subsequent dreams, she had been getting images of the actual abuse and perpetrator. It has caused anxiety and fear, but she has not regressed into a serious depression or suicidal ideation. Therefore, I thought it necessary to move into this very sensitive area, which will complete her personal healing and give her insight into the collective nature of sexual abuse problems in the general society today.

(T): In your dreams you're starting to see what happened to you. I mean the abuse when you were a little girl.

(P): It was awful. Painful. Shameful. I tried to make myself ugly. If I could have been uglier, then it wouldn't have happened. Would it?

(T): Remember, this is a vampire energy. I don't think that pretty or ugly has anything to do with it.

(P): You mean that the vampire doesn't care about looks?

(T): I think that the vampire is a spiritual entity. I think that spiritual entities are looking for spirit.

(P): Why my spirit? Why a little girl who had never hurt anyone? Why? All I can ask is why (*tears are flowing*).

(T): That's probably it. You said it. They are looking for purity. Innocence. That way they can project their poison onto the innocent child and at the same time try to turn the innocence into this evil entity.

(P): You mean they have a plan? I could become like them?

(T): Not anymore. You are gaining conscious knowledge of the vampire. Once you can see him, it's very difficult for him to possess you. You are also in the process of letting the energy go or transforming it.

(P): I don't want to transform it. I just want to be done with it.

(T): That's fine. Right now, you want to stop hurting. For now, that's what we'll do.

I hand her a box of tissues in a very slow and soft manner. At this point, it is best to let the process slow down. Continuing in order to deal with the bigger existential/spiritual issues could be devastating. It is time to create a stronger container for the patient. Patience is everything at this point and there must not be any rush to get at what the therapist might see as interesting material.

(T): Let's stop here. It's important to do only a little at a time. It can really hurt you if we do more. Let's put a circle around this and don't talk about it outside of this healing circle, okay? It's not that we're keeping secrets like vampires. It's just that I know that this is enough for now and we will get to it later. (*I bring a container with burning sage slowly toward her. I tell her that I will be going around her with the smoke in order to form a protective shield. She agrees and stops crying. The smoke is thick in the room, and she motions the smoke toward her heart.*)

(P): That's much better. That vampire stuff kinda freaked me out. The sage really helps. So, I shouldn't talk about this outside of here?

(T): Right. If you try to deal with this outside of here, then as you can see you'll be out of the smoke container. It should be done in a place where someone knows how to do this. I know how to do this, and I know that if it isn't contained, you can get hurt. It's not necessary for you to get hurt. You've suffered enough.

It is important that the Healer acknowledge the ability to contain the vampire. Therapists who do not feel competent to do this should not try these interventions, because the process easily can get out of control and the patient can be further abused. If the patient is abused by the Healer in this way, the patient may never seek help again and therefore be doomed to a life of suffering from this terrible pain. It is a huge responsibility that the Healer has toward the patient in this most critical moment. Also, there are different schools of thought that believe that a male therapist is not the right person to work with a female who has been sexually abused. Over the years, I have found that as long as the Healer is willing to deal with the spiritual entities, the work can be done by a male. Also, I tell patients that since the injury was done by a male, as in this case, the healing also should come from a male. The opposite can be true if the perpetrator is a female. In reality, if the Healer has integrated and is working toward integrating his own male and female energy, the gender issue does not have to become debilitating to the process. The reason I bring up the therapist gender issue is that there are many in our field who vehemently defend gender matching in these cases.

Sacrificing the Scapegoat

In the next sessions, the patient will be navigating in some very difficult psychological waters. We are going to work toward healing the deep injury caused by the sexual abuse. In working with sexual abuse, it is important to remember that this is an intergenerational problem and that the healing needs to take into account all of those who have suffered this type of spiritual intrusion.

> *Undoubtedly there will be readers who are victims of sexual abuse and are not therapists and not in therapy. The discussion that follows deals with archetypal material that may be difficult to integrate without qualified assistance. I caution these readers to please find a therapist, minister, Traditional Healer, or someone else who can guide them through this process. It shouldn't be done without assistance.*

(P): The last time you said something about how I suffered enough. I had a dream in which an old woman also told me that. Something about how I don't have to keep paying for what happened. Kinda went along with what we were talking about.

(T): Good. So, the dream is saying it's okay to talk about this. This means that you're strong enough to deal with some parts of the abuse that happened.

> *Care must be taken in the choice of words here. It is important to keep her from identifying with the abuse. Instead, this choice of words lets her know that an event or events happened that have caused a lot of pain. The fact that events happened can let her have more objectivity and ability to deal with the difficult material.*

(P): It happened all right. Since ages 7 to 9. It kept happening. It really makes me mad. I didn't deserve to be treated like that by my stepfather. Why couldn't I just have a regular stepfather like everyone else? I lost so much of my life already because of all this.

(T): Two years of being wounded, that's a long time. You must have felt so helpless.

(P): That's not the word for it. There was no one to talk to because no one would believe it. He was a very respected person in the community.

(T): You said that you lost so much life. That also can change and heal, you know.

(P): I don't see how. What's done is done. I lost my youth and cannot ever get it back.

(T): When you say it like that, you could be right.

(P): How else could I say it?

(T): You could offer your suffering to help yourself and others now.

(P): You're kidding? I don't want to help anyone with what happened.

(T): Maybe not now. It's just a thought.

(P): I'm so tired of all this. Being sick all the time doesn't help either.

(T): What kind of sickness are you talking about?

(P): Well, the diabetes. The blood pressure. Weight problems.

(T): Any of what are called "female problems"?

> *I ask this question because over the years many of the patients I've worked with in this context have had serious gynecological problems, many of which have resulted in surgical procedures such as hysterectomies and other major intrusive processes. I have gained insight regarding the relationship between these physical conditions and abuse. There appears to be a correlation in the patients I have seen over the years in the area of physical conditions and sexual abuse. The following session material will illuminate this. Again, this may appear different at least, and weird at worst, but the psyche can deal with primitive images better than our modern egos.*

(P): Oh, God, yes. You name it, I've had it. Literally some of it I don't have anymore. I mean some of my female parts or organs or whatever they call them.

(T): Traditionally at this point, an old woman should be asking you this stuff. We don't have an old woman to talk to you so I'll have to go into that role.

> *The reason I bring up this issue into the discussion is that in most Native communities it is still the place of elder women to discuss the so-called "female problem" area. I rarely have had access to an old woman who is adept at doing this, so I have had to fill that role myself. It is important that the therapist have an understanding and relationship with the inner old woman if this area is going to be dealt with as I'm discussing here. This requires study, meditation, active imagination, and permission from the dreamtime to go into this realm. I have been fortunate that in my process the psyche has given me images that have given me the permission to take on this role.*

(P): You? An old woman? Wow, that should be interesting.

(T): Well, I'm not going to put on an old dress and all . . . (*laughter*).

(P): That would be really interesting . . . (*more laughter*).

(T): Indeed it would. I'm sure that the inner female can relate to your inner male and somehow all this will make some sense. It really does, you know.

(P): Okay. So far, even the weird stuff you said, or what seemed weird at first, ended up making sense.

(T): Some of that stuff is pretty weird even to me, you know? But it's old knowledge, ancestral knowledge. It's not just Indian knowledge. White folks also know this stuff, except they have really forgotten it.

(P): White people? They know this?

(T): Yeah. It goes way back in their culture.

The issue of intercultural wounding is important. People need to know that the oppressors also have Original ways and through their own wounding process they have lost these. This type of discussion helps to heal issues of anger that the patient may harbor against White folks and engender a spirit of forgiveness.

(P): Oh. Guess it makes sense. They're just people too.

(T): So, what type of problems?

(P): Started with all kinds of weird period things. Bleeding a lot ever since I was young. My period never worked the way it's supposed to.

(T): Lot of bleeding. That sounds pretty serious. Wonder what that could be about?

Here's a Columbo-type question that will take the patient into deconstructing some of her physical problems in light of the injury that she received through the abuse as a young girl. Again, this is an important step for her to gain objectivity about her physical health and not to internalize that she somehow is a defective Indian in the physical sense also.

(P): Maybe I got hurt by the abuse. But the doctors said I was okay. Well, physically anyway. Yeah, right. All that bleeding and it's okay. Never really believed that.

(T): If you were physically okay, then it must have been something else. What controls all the bleeding and all that goes with your period?

(P): Guess the brain, glands, the mind, like that.

(T): When you were abused, did the abuse just hurt your body?

(P): No. It hurt everything. It still hurts, but not my body.

(T): Seems like the person that did this, hurt your spirit, your soul also. I've been told by some holy people that this is like sorcery. Especially when it's done to a sacred little one. All children are sacred, you know.

(P): I've heard that teaching a lot.

(T): He injured you in your body, mind, and soul.

(P): Yes . . . (*She starts crying. We sit quietly for about 2 minutes. I reach for the sage and burn smoke close to her in order to keep the spiritual container intact.*)

(T): This smoke will help to keep you safe in this circle. The spirit of the perpetrator is listening to what we're saying. Sometimes the spirit doesn't want to let go either.

(P): You're kidding. That sonofabitch is here? That mother fucker. I hate him. What he did. May he rot in hell.

(T): He probably has been. (*At this point, I agree in order to be able to go back to the area of the physical problems. The perpetrator will be revisited off and on until she can literally expel his energy from her psyche.*)

(P): I'm glad.

(T): Let's talk about the bleeding. What does blood mean to you?

(P): Hmmm. No one has ever asked that. I can see that's a pretty big question. Boy, blood. Hmmm. Blood is everything really. It's life itself. It's part of Creator.

(T): Seems like you know quite a bit about blood. Remember that time we talked about the scapegoat?

(P): Long time ago? Well, seems like a long time. It was only about 2 months ago. Yeah, something about the goat being sacrificed through no fault of his own. Poor goat. Goat ribs sure are good though . . . (*laughter*).

(T): They are. Haven't had some in a while myself. Well, remember there was a sin someone committed and in order to get rid of the sin, or bad thing, the sin was put on the goat's head, and then the goat was killed and burned on an altar. Kinda making a smudge offering out of the goat.

I'm making mythological connections between the goat and the idea of smoke as an offering much in the same way that we have done in the session. This will help the patient realize how she has been sacrificing herself and taking on the guilt of the perpetrator, which is a huge leap in insight and awareness.

(P): So, what are you saying? Sounds like you are kinda saying that I'm the scapegoat or something. That is really something. Is that what you're saying?

(T): I'm saying and asking. What I say is not as important as the connections that you're making right now. If I say it, who knows? It could be just my own idea. I believe that is how it happens though. I mean you being the scapegoat and all.

This is not an attempt to dodge the question as is customary in thera-
peutic circles. I answered the question pretty directly, and I also allowed
space for her own insight. The patient makes the connection, but this is
such a strange notion that it requires instant validation. Otherwise, the
patient will let go of the insight and her ego will come up with some other
socially acceptable construct to explain what she has been going through.
This type of ego intrusion has not been helpful to the patient and it is im-
portant to move around this type of ego thinking toward a mythological
or spiritual awareness of what actually is going on. After all, she has been
sacrificing through her suffering for many years already, and all of ego's
ideas have been useless. She continues to lose body parts and eventually
her life will be at stake, as it already has been with the suicidal ideation.
Transformation is possible only through these so-called primitive images
that fuel the transforming process and push ego notions to the side. Of
course, it is important to then engage ego into the new way of doing its
job through the understanding of these mythological views of so-called
reality. Ego then can be in service of spirit instead of itself.

(P): So, I have been taking on the sins of my stepfather? Shit. You
     have to be kidding. I don't want to take on his shit. God damn
     it!

(T): Yes, you have. Remember all the guilt you felt as a little girl?
     Feeling dirty and useless. Like you brought it on to yourself,
     especially since no one would have believed that it wasn't your
     fault? You took on his guilt and shame. It gets passed on, you
     know. Who knows where he got his guilt and shame. Some-
     thing happened to him to make him this way. I'm not saying
     this to say he's not responsible. It's just that you need to know
     that this energy gets transmitted just like the vampire bite. He
     was bitten, and he turned into a vampire and bit you. Now, we
     are stopping this and you are going to be well. Interesting how
     in this process you also are healing the vampire.

(P): Well, that's not what I want to do. I just want to be okay.

(T): I know. Right now, that's not the main task, as you say. See
     how your guilt may have led to your sacrificing of the very es-
     sence of who you are as a woman?

(P): What do you mean by that?

(T): Well, the vampire was a man. And the poison he put in you
     caused you to sacrifice your physical woman. I mean what you
     could identify or what makes you a woman. When you had the
     hysterectomy.

(P): Oh, my God. You mean that somehow that was part of all this?

(T): It seems so. Again, going back to the scapegoat. The goat is placed on the altar and then the blood sacrifice is done. You also were placed on the altar and then you gave your blood and body to balance out the sin.

(P): How do you mean? There was no altar. Just the hospital and I was out during the whole thing.

(T): You were on a modern altar, but it's still an altar. The surgeon's table is the altar and the surgeon was the priest. I bet you the surgeon was a man even, eh?

(P): You're right. Most of them are. Why is that important?

(T): The soul injury was committed by a man. Men in this culture have been pretty messed up for some time. The priest then is one of the collective of men and he was part of the sacrificing energy. I'm sure he was nice enough, and he had no clue. As far as he's concerned, this was just one of the many procedures he did that week. He actually would think that what we're talking about is complete insanity and bullshit.

(P): That's the truth. Would like to see his face around this kinda talk.

(T): Now, I'm not saying that all of these procedures are wrong or anything like that. What I'm trying to tell you is that because you already had one and with your history you might as well try to understand what it means that you lost your physical womanhood on the surgeon's table. If you didn't have this history, it would mean something else, I'm sure.

(P): So, everything means something, huh? It's like everything can be interpreted like a dream. I mean even small things that we don't think about. This makes life a lot more interesting. Even eating lunch and what happens around you then. Wow, this is trippy shit.

At this point, the patient is shifting her perspective into a more mytho-logical/existential one. Instead of seeing herself as a victim, she is finding interest in all aspects of her life. This is critical for all of us. No matter how comfortable our lives are, the truth is that we are moving toward old age, sickness, and death, as the Buddha taught. We can move into that area of our lives as victims or as warriors that have an understanding and wisdom of the essence of the moment and how this is related to our over-all life. This can be expressed by the Ericksonian concept of generativity versus despair: The conflict faced in old age in which the person either de-spairs due to a life that has not been lived well, or lives as a wise elder who still contributes to the community and society. (Erickson, 1980)

(P): This past week, I had a dream. In the dream, I had a baby. Weird, huh, because I can't have babies. But there I was with this most beautiful baby. She was the most amazing baby and there was such a feeling of love.

(T): That is wonderful. Babies are a really good sign of good things.

(P): Yeah, this one especially.

(T): Of course. It's your baby. The baby right there (*pointing at her*).

(P): What? You mean me (*smiling half shyly*)?

(T): Yes. The spirit has given you a gift. It is the reborning of your-self. You have given birth to the new you. All the possibilities for your new life without the vampire's poison. Your new sa-cred self.

(P): That is really a good thought. I felt so good after the dream. I actually feel real good right now. I haven't felt like this, gee, not ever really. You know I still hate him, but not the same way. It's kinda a pitiful hate. I don't think I would kill him now. I never thought this would ever change. I mean I don't want anything to do with him, but it's not like before.

(T): I can see that. You're a different person. Everything you do and think is different. Eventually, even this way of feeling to-ward him will change.

In subsequent sessions the patient continues to improve and make plans for her future. The relationship with the perpetrator also changes through the appearance of the perpetrator in dreams. Eventually, she is able to forgive him and have a new relationship with him in the dreamtime.

Brief Discussion of the Case

This case was very complex and the interventions cited above are small portions of the "breakthroughs" that occurred during the course of sev-eral months of treatment. Readers should be aware that the subtext is full of interventions, including problem-solving, supportive, insight, psycho-analytic, Jungian, and other Western approaches that are not delineated here. The Western interventions rely on eradicating pathology, while the model I am presenting relies on relating to energies with consciousness in a manner that will bring harmony to the person's life. I realize that I have made this point before, but I believe that it bears repeating; these interventions must be used only when the unconscious of the patient is ready to integrate them and sufficient ego strength is present. Please, do not go forward and throw these interventions at patients who do not have an adequate mythological understanding. Patience in developing this understanding with the patient is actually more important than the interventions themselves. Interventions without proper nurturing of the ego can be disastrous for the patient, and serious de-compensation, as in a loss of ego integrity, can occur.

CONCLUSION: PAIN AND THE SPIRIT OF HEALING

I always tell patients that the pain that they are experiencing already contains the "spirit of healing" within it. This is not a simple reframing, as is common in cognitive therapies. Spirit of healing must be understood within an Aboriginal perspective in which all of what we see or experience as reality has a dual nature. It follows that the greater the suffering, the greater the capacity to heal and continue to live in a manner that is in harmony with healing entities. Therefore, the profound suffering of individuals and the collective suffering of Native People can be seen as having an incredible power to transform the immediate situation as well as the world. Patients who realize that their suffering is not in vain can gain a meaningful existential connection to their life and to the lives of other human beings. In actuality, suffering is never completely alleviated for any of us as long as we stay attached to the world of illusion and ignorance. Therefore, most healers and therapists working in this context have a long way to go in the search and healing of their own souls. With this in mind, how do we help patients when in reality we are in need of the same help we are offering? It would be very easy to become paralyzed by this question and rationalize our inability to pursue this work because we all fall short of being enlightened. The task is to know how "pitiful" we are and with this humility to try to do the best we can in the face of these alarming spiritual forces that threaten to dismember our relatives, whom we call patients, and in the healing process threaten to dismember the unprepared Healer.

CHAPTER 7

Community Intervention

> Their ideal is to be men; but for them, to be men is to be oppres-
> sors. This is their model of humanity. This phenomenon derives
> from the fact that the oppressed, at a certain moment of their
> existential experience, adopt an attitude of "adhesion" to the op-
> pressor. Under these circumstances, they cannot consider him
> sufficiently clearly to objectivize him—to discover him outside
> themselves as oppressed is impaired by their submission in the
> reality of the oppression. At this level, their perception of them-
> selves as opposites of the oppressor does not yet signify engage-
> ment in a struggle to overcome the contradiction; the one pole
> aspires not to liberation, but to identification with its opposite
> pole. (Freire, 1990, p. 33)

IT STANDS TO REASON and intuition that the problems dealt with in individual and smaller settings also must be present in the larger collective community settings. We could focus on treating all the individuals one at a time and in time the whole community also would be healed. This seems like an outrageous idea, given the human suffering that would occur in the time it would take to solve problems. Therefore, we at least should attempt to discover and implement some solutions that may have wider efficacy and not take a millennium to ameliorate the problems that cause the suffering. Of course, I refer to suffering in the most common and relativistic way. The ultimate cause of suffering is our attachment to situations; being able to stop clinging and let go would be the absolute solution. Given that we are not fully enlightened, awakened beings, able to be unaffected by circumstances, I will discuss some solutions that may be effective in our relative world.

During the past few years, there has been a heightened awareness of historical trauma in Indian country. There is still a lot of work to be done in this area, but the fact that the ideas of historical trauma are reaching many of the social/behavioral health providers in Indian country is indeed encouraging. The work that needs to be done in our communities includes an aspect of healing from the issues discussed in previous chapters, as well as the reification of Native cultural forms at all personal and political levels. Knowledge of the trauma and how it affects the day-to-day life of community members still needs to reach the roots of the community and the community leadership. Unfortunately, much of the leadership in Indian country is preoccupied with other worthwhile issues, including economic development.

IS RESEARCH THE ANSWER?

Where to start is not a simple or rhetorical question. Many times, I have been asked to go to a community and do some type of community intervention. Requests for interventions are usually this nebulous because many of the people who are seeking help for their community do not really know what is needed. The problems have not been clearly delineated by the community or by our profession so far.

One of the main problems with our profession, which abounds with consultants who go into communities to try to help, is that the micro in our profession gets reflected in the macro. Consultants who pathologize individual patients in their practice will do the most logical thing imaginable; they will pathologize the collective situation or community as well. What else are they going to do with training received from a culture that perceives problems and suffering from a purely Western perspective? In essence, if all you have is a hammer, then you will use the tool at hand.

Research has become a favorite hammer for our profession and for funding sources at all levels of government. Researchers go into communities equipped with Statistics 101 through 505 and use this hammer on everything in sight. Not only that, but after they have hammered the psyches of the community with irrelevant instruments, they fly off to crunch their data and to publish their work in journals that most of the communities don't even know exist. This type of research has been categorized by some community members as "helicopter research." Just as a helicopter touches down, takes off vertically, and disappears as if no one had ever been there, the researchers come and go, with few positive effects for the research "subjects."

Presently, there is a new buzz word adopted by researchers that allows them to rationalize their research activities in communities: "participatory research." The idea behind this research method is that somehow the community is more involved in the research and thus the research is more meaningful and useful to the community. Unfortunately, the participatory research team continues to be comprised of academicians who have been immersed in Western training. Root metaphors of the questions that they use come mainly from Western thought; therefore, the Native community is removed from the research at the very beginning. At this point, some Columbo-type questions would be in order: If all the questions are immersed in a Western root metaphor, what kind of answer can we expect? How come the problems seem to get worse when all this help and resources are being expended?

I believe that participatory research should engage the root metaphor or most basic understanding of the life-world of the people being researched. The development of instruments used in the research needs also to be participatory, and validation should be in the control of those who have knowledge of these metaphors. I have yet to hear an alcohol researcher ask a group of people about the "spirit of alcohol." Yet, when this concept of alcohol has been discussed in treatment settings with many patients over many years, they all wonder why no one has ever talked about alcohol in this way. The fact that these root metaphors are not considered valid by researchers in the community only adds to the existing cultural disintegration. When researchers assume that their description of phenomena and their worldview is the only valid means of understanding, it becomes apparent that the purpose of the research is not for community healing. When the research is of a purely Western form, we have a neo-colonial activity being imposed on a community that is already suffering from historical trauma brought on by colonial processes. I must state that some researchers are beginning to develop "true" community research, but these are few at this time and their work has not made it into the body of literature. Research journals, which rely on referees, may have a difficult time allowing such literature to emerge, at least in the very near future. Most research journals still adhere to stringent Western empiricism that is not friendly to community researchers who may not be operating in that paradigm.

INTERVENTIONS WITH NATIVE COMMUNITIES

So, I ask again, where do we start? I can speak only of where I begin when I go into a community to do an intervention. Interventions usually are requested by someone in the community who has read some of the heresies that I have written. A social services person usually contacts me and solicits my visit, and the following conversation ensues:

Community Worker (CW): We would like you to come here to
    help us with our community problems.
Consultant (C): What kind of problems?

(CW): We have a lot of community dysfunction, alcohol, drugs, and such.

(C): I really don't know too much about your community. I'm sure there's someone there who can be of more help than me.

It is important that consultants do not believe that they actually have any answers. I try to convey in the conversation that my only task, if there is to be one, is to offer a process whereby the specific issues of that community can emerge. If specific issues can emerge, then specific answers will follow.

(CW): Right now, there's a lot of infighting among ourselves. The social services people aren't getting along with the docs. The tribal council is not being supportive, and they have other agendas. Our youth are in trouble, and no one seems to see any of this. (*I must stress that not all communities are in this category. There are some progressive communities that are making strides in solving these problems. I usually am contacted by the communities that need more assistance.*)

(C): Sounds like pretty big problems. Why do you think there's so much infighting?

A stupid-sounding question to start the process of deconstruction by applying conscious awareness into the nature of the problem. Hopefully, this process of questioning will begin to bring consciousness of the effects of historical trauma and internalized oppression that are at the center of the issue. By doing this, we won't have to pathologize the individuals who are responsible for the splitting or the dysfunctional systems that are in existence in this community.

(CW): It's something that has been going on for a long time. People's memories go way back. Even though they remember when things got bad, no one seems to know why things are the way they are.

(C): I wonder if this were 1491 whether we would even be having this conversation.

This is a question I ask frequently to community groups when I present to them. The question encourages people to think about what may have occurred to make things so drastically different in the present. The intent is not to romanticize the past, but to juxtapose one historical era with another. It doesn't matter that things were not perfect in pre-Columbian times. Conditions are much worse now, and there is a reason for this. The reason that stands out in my mind is the colonization process.

(CW): Probably not. But then again a lot has happened since, eh?
(C): Like what?

> *This question is asked in order to get the community person to reflect on the specific history of the community. All Native communities are different with respect to history and the level of trauma experienced. The community must become aware of its tribal trauma as well as the collective trauma of all other Original People. This awareness will allow for very specific interventions to be developed. The interventions will work only in the particular community and cannot be generalized to other groups.*

(CW): Well, you know. All the stuff that happened to Indian people. All the genocide. All the pain. The loss of language, culture, and our ways.

(C): I realize that a lot of stuff happened to Indian people all over. Right now, it would be important for you to find the specifics of what happened in your area.

(CW): That would really be something. That would be hard to do, because not a lot has been written on our small tribe.

(C): There may be other ways of finding out.

(CW): Like what?

(C): There's bound to be some older people who remember stories that were passed on to them by their grandparents and such. At times, this type of information is much better than what the anthropologists have recorded. There's always a bias in the historian, you know.

(CW): I see. I can start asking some of the other community workers if they know anyone who may remember some historical stuff. This could get interesting. Once we get all this history stuff, then what do we do with it?

(C): Then you have the stuff that you can use to do a community assessment. You can start understanding why things are the way they are in your community. At some point, you will have to present the historical material to the community. That's where it will get gnarly. The healing work will be difficult and painful. Without the historical honesty, though, it's hard to even start doing any of this.

Preparation for community healing is critical. Many times, community representatives will ask for help with a conference because they have heard that another community has had success with such events. It is important that the community's specific traumas be delineated first in order for the intervention to be relevant. It is useful to speak in general of the historical trauma, and no one would fault the attempt at healing with this approach. However, I have found that communities, like individuals, have their own set of traumas that result in particular symptoms that need to be dealt with very specifically.

For instance, some communities have had more direct contact with the military than others. There are communities like the Lakota, Cheyenne, and other Plains tribes that have had a long-standing military struggle at great cost of life and homeland. On the other hand, there are communities that settled quickly and were spared some of the genocide inflicted on the more resistant tribes. Some communities have suffered severe trauma resulting from the insults that have occurred to the land. Other communities have been profoundly affected by the residential boarding school era. One trauma, not often discussed, is termination: when the government unilaterally decides that the tribe is no longer a self-standing nation and can no longer have a government-to-government relationship with the U.S. government. Tribal termination is experienced as a severe injustice and betrayal. Of course, all communities have suffered all of these traumas to some extent. In the assessment, one needs to discover the source of the present-day problems that are keeping the community from becoming healthy.

Interventions cannot be "cook-booked" for individuals, much less for a whole community. If you become the consultant to help with the impact of intergenerational trauma in a community, it is very important that you are honest about what you actually can do. There is no way that a consulting "evangelist" simply can do a "tent revival" meeting, save everyone, and ensure that they don't backslide once he leaves the community. To be effective, the consultant must help the community obtain the tools to continue the process of community healing in the long run. The following important areas should be addressed by this process:

1. Raising awareness. The community must become aware of its historical context and understand how it has arrived at the present-day situation. Therefore, a process that facilitates discovery of community history needs to be developed. Historical discovery can be done through literature reviews as well as oral tradition. Both sources of information should be used to validate the data that emerge. The community must be in control of its own destiny in all of these activities.

Care should be taken in this process to let the community know the purpose of uncovering some very painful history. The community should understand that healing is the purpose. This process is not to be used solely for the purpose of inciting hatred of White people or to rub salt in the soul wound.

2. Devising a plan to continue the healing process. The plan must include a raising of awareness as to the roots of the community's history. Understanding the historical context in the present-day problems will help greatly in decreasing the community's identification with the problems. Consciousness raising and specific interventions dealing with historical trauma and internalized oppression should be part of an overall community healing process. These interventions must be delivered early on in the process.

Health and tribal government systems and infrastructure that are in existence must be modified by changing some of the colonial forms of government to more Native forms. This is necessary in order to effectively deal with the types of situations that the consciousness raising undoubtedly will create. For instance, providers working in behavioral health settings must undergo extensive training in addressing historical issues in a manner that does not pathologize the community. These staff members must be ready to meet with the community on a regular basis in order to evaluate the ongoing development and intervention projects that are to be implemented. Some of these projects will include discussion with elders and leaders in the area of community revitalization. In addition to discussion with elders, the whole community needs to be brought together for meetings, including traditional forms of getting together as well as Western interventions designed to deal with present problems such as addiction and violence.

3. Thoroughly evaluating tribal government administrative systems. Evaluation of tribal structures will not be an easy task because some administrative structures are colonial in nature and will resist change. It is critical to point out to tribal government administrators that perhaps their administrative process is a colonial one and that there may need to be some changes in the way the political system operates. Administrative systems are the most resistant to change because most of these systems are steeped in bureaucratic inertia caused by colonization. In addition, it is risky for health program and tribal administrative staff to go against the status quo due to fear of job loss and other systemic retaliatory devices. These obstacles can become almost insurmountable, and this part of the task may take years. Honesty at the beginning of the process is important to avoid raising false expectations. Community "change agents" need to be committed to the long-term solutions and have patience that not even Job could have imagined.

Changes often are accepted most readily in a community's health delivery system, because most health systems have been brought in from outside the community. The primary goal is to achieve some change, any change, so that the community will realize that change in itself is not a bad thing. Many times, people become paralyzed by the mere idea of change because things have been done in the same manner year after year, even though they have not been very effective.

One model that is showing some effectiveness in some communities is the organization of a series of community healing conferences. These healing conferences are spread across several years, and some of the ideas in this book have been included in them. The conferences begin with awareness and diagnosis of the problem. Community people must take a courageous inventory of their history. In the beginning, there may be splits between different factions in the community, but these can be dealt with through an honest look at history.

ADDRESSING RELIGIOUS DIFFERENCES IN NATIVE COMMUNITIES

A common faction or discord is that between the "Traditionals" and the "Christians." Due to issues of internalized oppression, people acting on the illusion of difference will oppose one another due to religious differences. Without going into a deep theological discussion, it can be asserted that the beliefs of Christians and Traditional Native People can be compatible and do not necessarily conflict. Historically, harsh judgments have gone back and forth between the two religions and this has served only to alienate individuals from one another as well as divide families and communities. Both Traditional practitioners and Christians have developed a reactive mind-set, making it difficult to get through to either side and restore harmony. I have witnessed these conflicts several times and have had some success in bridging this gap. The following consulting dialogue is typical:

> Christian (CH): All of this stuff that you are talking about is
>   against the Bible, you know.
> Me (M): How so?
> (CH): When you use smoke and stuff, how do we know who
>   you're praying to?
> (M): I do it in a good way. Probably praying to the same person
>   you're praying to.
> (CH): When you did that, I had to go to my room and pray and
>   read the Bible.
> (M): That's good. I'm glad that you are practicing your faith. You
>   know what? There's no need for you to go to your room to do

that. Maybe tomorrow, if you want, you can start the morning session of the conference with a prayer and a reading from the Bible.

(CH): What? You serious?

(M): Yeah. I think it would do us all good to have a good prayer.

(CH): I could ask some of the relatives to help. Maybe sing a hymn too.

(M): That would be really good. You know, I think if Christ were at this conference, he would really like what's going on right now.

(CH): What about the other people? What are they doing? I mean the ones that go to the sweat-lodge at night?

(M): I'm not going to speak for God or anything, but if Christ were here I think he would sing a hymn with you and also sing a hymn in the sweat-lodge. I don't think he would care what the prayer sounded like as long as it was from the heart.

(CH): Never thought of it that way. Makes sense.

(M): I want to tell you something. This will sound a little weird. I think that Christ was one of the Original Sundancers. He hung on the tree just like the Sundancers.

(CH): Hmmm. That's interesting. Never really saw it like that. Maybe we're hassling about stuff that shouldn't matter that much. Who's to say what the true way is. Or what is the only way. It's just that we've been brought up like that.

(M): Why do you think that is? (*By now, the reader should be able to fill in the rest here. This Columbo-type question is intended to get the person to trace the history of the rigid belief system that he's been caught up in.*)

(CH): Well, it has been like that for some generations. Guess it started about the time that the priests came into the community about 150 years ago.

(M): Up to that point, what was going on in the community?

(CH): People were living and praying in the old way.

(M): Was that okay? I mean, the fact that your ancestors were praying in the old way?

(CH): Yah, I mean they knew what they were doing. They were all good people.

(M): So, if people pray in the old way now, could that be okay?

(CH): This is something. I never saw it like this. Guess so. I mean it should be okay.

(M): Maybe Christ would appreciate a little cedar in the fire to clear the air some. You know they use smudge in the church also, so it seems as if smoke is a good thing when used in a prayer way.

(CH): They do, don't they? So, all this bickering is really something that is just separating us.

By now, the consciousness of this community leader is starting to change. I don't mean to imply that it will happen in a few minutes. This usually takes persistence, humor, and understanding of both Traditional and Christian teachings and lifestyle. The consultant must feel comfortable in both of these worlds, which are really just one world. Otherwise, the intervention should not be attempted, much in the same way that I have been cautioning the reader all along in this book.

HEALING THE LAND

Once community awareness has been raised, the community needs to design specific interventions to address its specific soul wound. One community I worked with was very concerned with some of the insults and injuries that had occurred to the land. I advised the people that they needed to go to the specific places on the land where the injuries occurred. These injuries could consist of direct assault of the land as in mining or deforestation. Soul wounding of the land also can occur when there is a massacre of human beings on the land. Basically, the land needs to undergo assessment and treatment in order to restore balance. It is difficult to restore balance to the community of human beings if the land's soul has been wounded and left unhealed.

This is a peculiar idea for psychology, which has objectified the land in the manner that Descartes speculated in his infamous "cogito ergo sum" statement. This very objectification of the land has allowed for the psyche of human beings to desecrate and wound the soul of the land. There are still people who live on the land and do not objectify the Earth. The pain of the land is their pain. As human beings, our sense mechanisms are the only way that the land, which makes up our body, can express the pain it feels through our/its consciousness. This may take some reflection, but if reflection and contemplation are given proper space, I'm sure that even the psyche that has accepted the illusion of separate existence realizes that this makes rational sense. Perhaps, rationality is just a by-product of the Earth's consciousness trying to become aware of itself through the psyche that humans have acquired from the Earth.

The notion of Earth consciousness is not just one that is shared by Original People. It is evident from Jung's Zarathustra seminars (Lecture 3, 1988) that Nietzsche's thinking reflected an awareness of Earth consciousness.

You probably noticed that peculiar expression, the "four square" body. The body is of course very much the earth, and "it speaketh the meaning of the earth" means that inasmuch as the body has produced consciousness, it produces the meaning of the earth. If you could give consciousness or a creative mind to a book for instance, or to any kind of object, it would speak its contents; give consciousness to wood and it speaks the meaning of wood; give it to stone it speaks the meaning of stone. . . . This shows that if one remains persistent in the hidden, unspoken purpose, then the very nature of the earth, the hidden lines in the earth will lead you. (p. 356)

In order to provide healing of the Earth, or "Earth therapy," some basic rules of natural law need to be observed. As in the case when one offends an individual, it becomes necessary to apologize and make some sort of amends. The Earth was subjected to a monumentally huge insult during the time of colonization. Not only was the Earth insulted by the violence against the human beings who are part of the Earth, but the Earth itself was subjected to injury by the thoughtless cutting, poisoning, and other atrocities committed in the name of progress and making money.

The destruction of culture was an injury sustained by the consciousness of the Earth, of the suffering experienced by human beings who lived on the Earth. Ceremonial forms of relating with the Sacred were literal projections of Earth consciousness that were carried out by the consciousness of the people. Objects became sacred as part of the communal use and practice, and became charged with "Earth spirit." Removal and destruction of such objects has had and continues to have a profound impact on the psyche of Original Peoples.

Therapeutic interventions with communities must take into account "Earth therapy" if the community intervention is to make any sense at all to the people involved. Ceremonial objects must be returned to their home where they once resonated with the Earth and community. Ceremonial objects that need to be returned include baskets, ceremonial pipes, bows, arrows, ceremonial clothes, and so on. The return of these objects becomes a charged issue for individuals and agencies who have them in their custody and actually believe that they own such objects. These ceremonial objects belong to the spirit of community and can be very useful in the re-integration of new Traditional forms.

In no way do I want to imply that by returning these ancient objects, we are to return to old ways that may not work in a modern society and world. Returning of objects and ceremonial forms is a means of healing for individuals and community. The return can facilitate the development of new ceremonies that will deal with issues such as the soul wound and internalized oppression. These objects are not tied to just one space and time. Ceremony transcends space and time. These objects can be used to take the individual consciousness across the barriers of space and time and heal ancestral as well as present-day soul wounding.

CONCLUSION: A SLOW PROCESS

Community intervention follows the same process as intervention with individual patients, as delineated in previous chapters. Problems of community addiction, sadness, abuse, and violence are manifestations of many individuals. Through the healing of individuals, the groundwork can be laid for the greater healing of the community. In essence, if even a small critical mass of healing can be generated in a few people, this will create a snowballing effect that can encompass the whole community in positive healing. Healing on a community level will require long-term commitment and patience and has to come from the community, because most consultants and health workers do not stay a whole lifetime in the community.

An example of the type of commitment required is exemplified by the 100 miles of trees that were planted in an ancient community. The trees take over 100 years to grow, but the community planted them anyway. One hundred years later, the descendants of these visionaries were able to enjoy the shade of a 100-mile path. Of course, the Original visionaries never got to see the results of their efforts. If you are attached to results, it is best that you stay out of community work unless you are equally attached to frustration. It is with this kind of intent and courage that community work must be approached.

CHAPTER 8

Clinical Supervision

There is no teacher, no student. At times teaching arises when the right conditions exist.

URING THE PAST 20 years, I have had the privilege to be a part of training 30 interns. Most who have trained with me have been White folks, and the process has been most interesting on both sides of the supervision equation. Interns are attracted to work in Native communities because they intuit that there may be something different in the experience. Many of the interns entertain fantasies of what Native life is like, and very early on in the experience they realize that this internalized romantic idea of Native People is completely wrong.

The initial stage of selecting interns has shown me how deeply some of the American fantasies of Native People are engrained in the American culture. Some students want to work in a Native setting so that they can learn about Native spirituality. Others have a more subconscious motivation of saving the Indians. This archetypal missionary psychology can be a disaster in a clinical setting where the problems require knowledge and treatment of historical trauma. There is no ideal intern, and the training process must facilitate the relationship between the intern and the patient with a wounded soul.

Clinical supervision has been difficult for some interns, especially in the beginning stages. Interns have been trained to expect certain things from their supervisors and for the most part they have a structure of supervision engrained into their psyches well ahead of any actual supervision. I must say that supervisors have had the same structures engrained into them. Further, by the time they become supervisors and have done supervision for a few years, these constructs have solidified and the supervisors perpetuate the routine Western-based and biased supervision. Even when supervision occurs in so-called minority settings, the actual event of supervision is skewed by Western empiricism, with some paternal observance of minority issues as they are believed to pertain to the "minority" patient. Of course, there are exceptions. I am referring to most clinical settings in our society and those societies that have embraced American standards.

Students usually come to their initial supervision sessions with a list of issues, including administrative concerns, about what type of cognitive therapy will work and how to diagnose their patients. Given that they have chosen to work in a Native setting, I attempt to offer as genuine an experience as possible regarding non-Western ways of thinking. It is my contention that if they can begin to deal with what may seem to be an irrational way of perceiving the world in a supervisory setting, then this will transfer to their work with patients. Many of the students have had difficulty with this approach, but only in the beginning.

A SAMPLE OF SUPERVISORY DIALOGUE

Recently, I was asked about my supervisory style during a supervision seminar that included all types of experts. I tried to be mindful of the question and the answer. After a few moments of deliberation, all I could come up with was that "my style is that I have no style," which was not exactly the answer they were expecting. I suppose that I could have come up with some interesting culturally competent theory that would have seemed more in line with the proceedings. However, I must hold that answer and try to expound on it in the best way I can in this section. In order to do so, it is best to give a sample of some supervisory dialogue.

> Supervisor (S): How are your cures going? (*Even though there is a huge difference between healing and curing, I use the term* cure *in order to provoke critical thinking on the part of the intern.*)
> Intern (I): Cures? I don't understand. What do you mean?
> (S): If you're not here to cure people, what are we doing?
> (I): It's my understanding that we just facilitate. We don't get too involved in the cure, if there is such a thing.
> (S): I sure hope there is such a thing; otherwise, it looks pretty grim for our patients. They're really suffering, and they need to be cured, you know.
> (I): I have some things I need to run by you. (*Intern starts to refer to a paper with notes on it.*)
> (S): You have this stuff written down? Like a laundry list or something?
> (I): Well, kinda. I just have to go through this systematic tally; otherwise, I might forget something.

(S): That wouldn't be such a bad thing. Did you ask your depressed patient if she dreamed anything?

(I): No. That's not something I ask ordinarily.

(S): How are you going to know what's going on? The patient obviously doesn't know; otherwise, they wouldn't be coming here. I don't know either . . . do you have it written on the list there?

The process is not adversarial as the words in this section may appear to be. There are a lot of pauses in my questions, and I make sure that I show through my affect and body language that this is not a situation in which the intern is in difficulty. It's a process of allowing for the epistemology of the intern to take a different turn and begin to explore another life-world in which things are not neatly sequenced as in a laundry list.

(I): Well, I did do an intake and wanted to discuss some of the issues that came up.

(S): Is the patient's soul wounded?

(I): Pardon me? I'm sure I heard you, but I don't understand.

(S): The depression. Where do you think this comes from? Is it a terrible long-standing depression?

(I): She's been depressed a long time.

(S): Have you heard of intergenerational trauma before?

I want to reiterate again that the line of supervision that I'm disclosing here is additional to the regular Western supervision that the intern receives. Many times, I defer the Western supervision to another supervisor in order to make sure that the interns complete their Western training. Most of the time, though, I work in both tracks and provide supervision in the areas in which most students in this country train, including assessment, diagnoses, and the different therapies that go with this. Therefore, what I'm presenting here is more of the subtext of the supervision process that students receive over a 6- to 12-month period).

(S): Where do you come from?

I purposely shift the topic to a nonsensical topic in order to keep the intern's ego from getting too involved in figuring out what is going on intellectually. It is frustrating to the students, because their train of thought has been derailed and they are not in control of the situation. I believe that it is critical that we never get so arrogant as to believe that we are in control of the forces that govern the psyche. Instead, these forces are in control, and we are merely trying to appease them with the use of good manners, as I have tried to explain in this book so far.

(I): What? What does this have to do with the depression of my patient?

(S): Is that how you learned how to talk where you come from?

(I): Huh? I guess . . . (*silence for a few moments*). Where I come from? No one has really asked that question before. I come from Ohio.

(S): Is that in the United States?

Obviously, a stupid Columbo-style question. This is used in order to throw the thinking process of this very highly intelligent student off the thinking track. Hopefully, this will serve to bring him to a place of heart in which compassion can flow and enhance his already superb intellect.

(I): Well, yes . . .

(S): (*I interrupt*). No need to answer; it's just a rhetorical question.

Now, the student is really confused because he does not have to answer the question at all. In his mind, he is trying to figure out why I asked it in the first place and perhaps wondering some about my abilities as a supervisor. This has gotten his ego to spend time on the situation, which in turn opens the door for his unconscious to be able to assimilate what actually is going on, that is, a deeper healing for the patient and the student that does not come from words. Instead, this type of healing comes from the life force that has its beginning in the heart.

(I): I'm confused. Where is this going?

(S): It's not going anywhere. It doesn't come from anywhere. All you have is just now.

(I): Huh? Can we get back to my patient? I really need to talk about that.

(S): That's what we're doing, I thought. Did your grandma teach you to talk that way about people?

(I): What way?

(S): You just said, "get back to my patient." Somehow, that implies that the patient belongs to you.

This is an important distinction for the student. He also must gain objectivity in the situation. The process belongs to the patient. We are there merely to offer some insight into how patients can gain balance and harmony in their life. At times, the symptoms may persist and then we assume that it's our fault for not being better Healers. This can be avoided if we acknowledge that the life process or karma belongs to the person who is living it. By offering an existential meaning to the situation, we are part of a great gift in the process that the patient finds herself in. This way of thinking in no way removes our responsibility for the process, but at the same time we can avoid the pitfalls that can cause severe burnout.

(I): I said that, huh? Everyone says that. Never really stopped to think about it. Guess we say a lot of stuff that we don't stop to think about.

(S): Yes. That is really the whole thing. I mean, to be aware of everything we say and why we say it. Words have power, you know. Awareness is the only thing that can keep us from messing things up.

(I): This is interesting.

(S): Wonder what your grandma would say to you now.

(I): I used to be close to her when I was young. Then life gets in the way and you lose track.

(S): It happens like that a lot. Maybe you need to call your grandma or write to her. Better yet, maybe you can go see her next time you are on vacation.

(I): I actually would like that.

(S): So, the patient you're seeing has been depressed for a long time?

(I): Most of her life.

(S): It could have started even before she was born.

This is an opening to get the student acquainted with intergenerational trauma. The steps are similar to the ones used in working with patients. In working with students, I assign reading to them in order to expedite the process. Fortunately, there is a growing body of literature in this area, and students can become familiar with the theory and some of the clinical applications quickly. In addition, workshops are given all over Indian country on the topic, and I encourage students to attend these trainings to get hands-on experience. This way, interns can gain the maximum exposure to direct healing and help more patients in their generally brief training period. I have found that students are very open to this and actually find it a respite from some of the usual clinical experience that they are subjected to in their training.

(I): That's interesting. I've heard something about this before, but it sounded so theoretical.

(S): Theory does have a way of being derived from real life. So, how are you going to cure the patient?

The use of the word cure *is very frustrating to students because they are not familiar with it. I purposely use it in order to facilitate discussion of the difference between curing and healing. Again, this confuses the ego and allows for a deeper insight into the healing work that we do.*

(I): Cure? We don't cure people.

(S): Well, I hope you didn't tell the patient that. I'm sure that she's expecting some kind of cure from you.

(I): No, I didn't say anything about it. In our training, we're taught that we just facilitate the process.

(S): Toward what?

(I): Hmmm . . . no one has really said. At least, I don't recall toward what.

(S): I'm no rocket scientist, but the word *facilitate* literally means "to make easier," eh? Easier how? Toward what?

(I): Maybe toward a better life? Or ease in symptoms. Lessen the depression in this case.

(S): If you're going to do that, it sounds like a cure to me. I mean if you're going to lessen the depression, that sure sounds like you are going to cure her. What if the symptoms don't decrease? You know all of our patients are going to die someday of something.

(I): What does that have to do with anything?

(S): It has everything to do with everything. If this patient stays depressed, does that mean you have failed her?

(I): Well, kinda.

(S): You know, there is a difference between curing and healing.

(I): Are you going to tell me or is this another one of your Zen Koans (*confusion techniques*) that have no answer.

(S): Koans, eh? Didn't really see it like that, but all Koans have an answer. The answer could be that there is no answer.

(I): That was good . . . (*laughing*).

(S): Okay. Healing has to do with harmony and balance of spirit. You could have the worst illness imaginable and still be healed. If you're sitting at the center of the universe, then you are healed. On the other hand, curing has to do with the removal of symptoms or disease, sickness, and such. This is the frustration of the Western medical model, that is, that it cannot cure the inevitable, because all patients are going to die. Only difference is that they may die without healing or still out of balance. With Native/Original Peoples' medicine, it is perfectly okay to die. But it is not okay to die out of balance with the forces that create life and death. See what I'm saying?

(I): Starting to. Kinda like an existential meaning?

(S): Kinda like that. Existential meaning with deep relationship to the forces of nature and natural law. Guess you could call it existentialism with an Aboriginal twist?

(I): So, this goes further than just meaning. Relationship with the actual natural law. Never got any of this in any of my coursework. Seems pretty important not just for Indian people. I think White folks could stand some relating to the life force or natural law.

(S): I agree. This is missing from the culture. That's why we're about to wipe ourselves out of existence. I mean existentially, in the purest form, if we are without relationship, we would be okay with this, right? I mean it would all have meaning, even if all is destroyed. All of this from one depressed patient. Amazing how one is everyone.

I say this in order to connect the student to the collective. Most Euro-Americans are very individualized and have lost connectedness to other people as well as to the Earth herself. It is critical that the student understand how nature and natural law relate to themselves through our consciousness. Of course, there is also discussion of interventions with the patient, but here I continue to discuss the subtext. I do not discuss the usual therapies because readers are assumed to be well versed in these, and, if not, there is a plethora of literature on Euro-American therapeutic strategies.

(I): So, how do I start relating more? I mean the way you're talking?

(S): How do you relate to anyone? In the beginning, there is etiquette, right? There are manners that are followed. We all know them intuitively. Well, same way with these relatives.

(I): What relatives?

(S): Healing relatives. They are your relations. They know you. They have been following you your whole life. How else do you think you have gotten into this field of becoming a Healer? They are in this room right now. They have been waiting for you to acknowledge them.

(I): This is a bit eerie. Somehow, I know that what you're saying is true. But it's weird. What do I do?

(S): Same thing you did when you met me. Say hello. (*At this point I light some sweet-grass and allow the smoke to gently move through the office. The student is very still and attentive.*)

(I): That smells nice. Kinda like pancake syrup or something.

(S): I thought I'd give your ancestors a nice welcome. Right now, they are happy that you are beginning to acknowledge them. I can almost hear your great great grandma saying, "Welcome to the circle, my grandson." That is really good.

(I): Somehow, that makes me so happy and sad at the same time. This is really a different kind of supervision. Never heard anything like this. Makes sense and I feel centered somehow knowing that these ancestors are watching and even helping. Wow, who can I talk to this about, though? Can't talk to just anyone without them thinking I'm crazy.

(S): You see, it's important that your ancestors know you so that they can relate to the ancestors that the patient is bringing in. All seven generations are involved in the healing process. If these folks don't know and relate to one another, then there are some gaps in the healing process. So, you need to keep enhancing this relationship with your ancestors so that they can keep helping you. Note your dreams. Feed them.

(I): Say what? You said, feed them?

(S): Yes, it's good manners to feed the spirits. Especially if you're on the healing path. You need to pay special attention to this etiquette. You know, you're not a civilian. You have to live by different rules. So, when you have lunch or dinner, just set aside tiny bits of food and drink that you are having and put these on the Earth with the intent that you are feeding your ancestors. They'll appreciate it and help you out with this patient and others. You might say they'll give you some extra supervision in this area.

CONCLUSION

This dialogue should give a flavor for how I do clinical supervision. I need to remind the reader that this aspect of supervision is additional to the usual supervisory issues that need to be dealt with. Interns bring in assessment and diagnostic data that need to be interpreted, and I assist them in this process. All of the other areas of clinical supervision are attended as specified by the requirements of the profession, such as amount of supervision, progress notes, report writing, and other administrative concerns.

I was hesitant to write this chapter because future students may read it and have some ready-made ego defenses to counter some of these confusion methods. After some reflection, I thought that it's fine if students have knowledge beforehand. In fact, this simply will encourage me to get more creative as I go along and perhaps come up with some interventions that will confuse even me. It actually happens all the time, because the spirit of Coyote is as infinite as the Coyote's howl from which all creation emerged, according to most mythologies of Original Peoples of Turtle Island.

It is interesting to note that all of the students I have supervised over the years become comfortable in this style of supervision in a very short period of time. The process is open to creativity, which usually is not the case in standardized supervisory models that are used in most graduate and postgraduate internship sites. I am optimistic that our professional overseers, such as the American Psychological Association, American Counseling Association, Social Workers Associations, and American Psychiatric Association, will be open to different approaches to training future professionals. The needs of our society are changing because we are becoming more multicultural, and this change will require that we change the manner in which we deliver very critical services to our various populations.

CHAPTER 9

Before Completion

It is more of a seeing than a looking. The flash of recognition is always a momentary thing—a turning of a moment into another as in sighing. The glimpse of sparkle on a shiny surface. The smell of a place; the taste and texture of thought, the point between the breath's coming in to its end and stating its going out. A quick somethingness—it eludes the fixed gaze, leaving only an impression. These are the moments we say need seizing if we are to ride the wind. Something cautions us; do not go looking for clouds in the closet, you'll not find your shoes in the sky. The trick of grabbing the wind is a sort of personal exploration for me. (Andy Curry, 1972)

THE I' CHING ends with hexagram 64. This hexagram (the six lines that make up a particular situation, obtained through chance tossing of coins or sticks, as described in Chapter 6) is entitled "Wei Ji" (before completion) and literally means not yet across the stream, or the stream has not yet been forded. It is with this insight in mind that this particular work will end, or rather not end because it is "before completion." It is important to me and to the reader that we understand that this work is merely part of a cyclical change that inevitably will need to continue changing. In the hexagram, all of the yang lines (solid lines) are in even-numbered places and all of the yin lines (broken lines) are in odd-numbered places. According to the I' Ching (Balkin, 2002), this is the exact opposite of how things should be. Even though the lines are placed incorrectly, the start of harmony is present. It is encouraging to know that natural processes are not judgmental and that all things follow a natural order. It is this natural order that should give us optimism in our day-to-day work of trying to heal individuals and communities. The completion of this cycle is not an end, but, in fact, is the beginning of a new way.

It is in this spirit that this book arrives at completion. I encourage the reader, Healer, student to realize that these words are to be taken only within the context of this moment. Once the moment passes, all is in renewal. Therefore, I hope that you will take these ideas, work with them, and improve on them as the moment of healing directs you. There is a lot of work yet to be done. We are barely scratching the surface of the human psyche, and it is critical that we keep an open mind for the integration of knowledge from a psyche with infinite capacity.

Most of the interventions discussed in this book are as old as the mountains themselves. There is nothing new discussed in these pages. Interestingly enough, these ideas cannot even be classified as culturally competent specific to the Original People of Turtle Island. I am sure that some questions may arise in the minds of readers who may be wondering, "What is this if it is not about cultural competence?" Is this a misrepresentation since the tone of the book is cultural competence?" Of course it is not a misrepresentation. Instead, this type of dialogue allows for fluidity and contradiction, which are integral to the world of Coyote and open-ended thought versus dogma. Most of these ideas are part of the human psyche and do not belong to any one group. Original People have existed throughout the world, and everyone on the planet is part of an Original People. There is only one Origin of all People.

In Chapter 7, I wrote about how Earth healing needs to occur in places where Original Peoples' souls were wounded. Since there is no separation between the wounded and the one causing the wound, it stands to reason that Earth healing will restore the souls of both the wounded and the perpetrator of the wounding. In a point in space and time, the relationship between the wounded and perpetrator took place on the Earth. The energy that was released in the process affected the Earth consciousness, and the psyches of both sides were involved in the wounding. Because Original Peoples have lived everywhere on the Earth, it stands to reason that the whole Earth needs to go through a healing process beginning with an apology from all of us human beings. The apology must be followed by a respectful relationship to the Earth that continues to nurture us despite what we have done to her.

Presently, there is an all-out assault on the Earth from those who seek to exploit resources for the simple purpose of greed and domination. How different would it be if these same people who wish to exploit the Earth would simply offer a gift to the Earth and ask permission to take the resources that the Earth has provided freely for all of us? I have an image of an oil baron going to the north slopes in Alaska and offering a prayer of thanksgiving to the Earth. During that prayer, the oil baron would leave a gift of tobacco or cornmeal and ask the Earth for a blessing of heat, lighting, and all of the benefits that can be derived from taking her oil. Then the oil would be distributed in a generous fashion so that the result of such an act would be a blessing and not a curse, as has been the case. Again, I merely speak of shifting metaphors, which would change the very consciousness of how we will continue to live on the Earth.

The issues discussed in this book have far-reaching implications outside of the therapeutic setting. Lack of cultural understanding or lack of cultural competence could be one of the most threatening concerns to humanity and the planet. The fact that different metaphors are part of the various factions and religions involved in daily systemic killing, should be considered in the solutions offered by those in power. It makes little rational sense to try to make peace, using a purely Judeo-Christian metaphor, with people who do not understand the metaphor as part of their day-to-day life-world.

It is with some sadness that I recently have become aware that our profession persists in adhering to Western ideology exclusively as part of what is considered to be the latest developments in psychotherapy. During the fifth "Evolution of Psychotherapy" conference, there will be no mention of the pioneers of cross-cultural work in the field. The fact that cross-cultural work is not seen as part of the evolution of psychotherapy in the West indicates to me how far we need to go in order to bridge supremist ideology that is firmly entrenched in our field. I feel it is considerably sadder to see that the program comprises people who are known masters in the field and remain silent. I infer from their silence that they are in agreement with the premise of the conference; that is, that psychotherapy is a Western Judeo-Christian-based discipline and we "coloreds" have no place at the table.

Another example of lack of cultural understanding and respect is having Western-based governments and diplomats negotiating with tribes that have had their own forms of government. This is similar to treating Original People with purely Western therapies. As has been discussed in this book, this type of approach is merely another form of colonization that imposes yet another instance of violence on our brothers and sisters who simply see the world in a different way. We need to become open-minded (in the metaphor of some Original People, the mind signifies the heart-mind) and realize that the Euro-American root metaphor for being in the life-world is not the only one or the correct one. It is simply one of many root metaphors that exist as part of the evolving of culture. Allowing relationships in the world to continue as they are will only expand human suffering, and the threat of total destruction will continue to loom on the horizon.

I believe that all of these religions, theories, and ideas are true. All of the constructs, as far as the Original People emerging out of the same psyche, appear to resonate with most cultural belief systems. Furthermore, the psyche is simply a part of the dream that continues to dream itself. Consciousness itself is a by-product and at the same time the genesis of this origin or matter that somehow, somewhere became aware of itself and now believes that the matter that has become brain matter is the ultimate knower. The simplest exercise in knowing will let us realize that somehow there is a knowing that is knowing the knowing of consciousness. I ask one last stupid Columbo-type question before I close with something my root teacher said about this: "Who or what is knowing the knowing?"

In my opinion, my Root Teacher Tarrence said it best.

> There has always been a dream. Every thing is still the dream. All that we call creation and Creator is the dream. The dream continues to dream us and to dream itself. Before anyone or anything was, there was a dream, and this dream continued to dream itself until the chaos within the dream became aware of itself. Once the awareness knew that it was, there was a perspective for other aspects of the dream to comprehend itself. One of the emerging dream energies, or formations of mind that came from the chaos of the dream and still remains in the dream as a way for the dream to recognize itself, is called "human beings." Human beings required a way to have a perspective and reference, and because of that, another energy emerged from the dream, and this is known today as time. It is from the two energies of dream and time that the third was given birth to, and that third one is known as the dreamtime. Dreamtime is also known as mind, which is by nature luminescent, empty, and pure. And the dreamtime mind is reflected by the emptiness of awareness. (Duran, 2000, p. 1)

The words of my teacher are beautiful and deep with meaning. Most of the issues discussed in this book have to do with the mind and how we relate to our minds. Most of the suffering that we encounter in our moment-to-moment life is directly related to the mind-state that we are in. It is indeed a deep comfort to realize that the mind is empty, luminescent, and pure. It is the nature of mind to have this empty purity, and no matter what mind-state makes its way across the mind landscape, it is impermanent and empty. Eventually all interventions become useless due to their own inherent emptiness.

In this book, I have presented some simple ideas that can be used to intervene in healing settings. These interventions are not purely clinical. Relationship with the natural order should be something that is done daily as part of being in the life-world. Even though many of us aren't aware of relating, there is a constant relating that occurs every time we take a breath. In that moment of noticing the breath we come into full relationship with all of the cosmic dream that continues to dream us. In that dreaming process, creation continues to unfold in a mysterious manner that eventually is not mysterious at all and is merely part of a natural process that creates, destroys, and recreates without any judgment or attachment. It just is.

May the Sacred Be Restored in Beauty
May the Sacred Be Restored in Beauty
May the Sacred Be Restored in Beauty
May the Sacred Be Restored in Beauty.

Aho!! Mi Takuye' Oyacin. All are my relatives.

References

Adler, G. (1984). *Selected letters of C. G. Jung.* Princeton, NJ: Bollingen Press.

American Psychiatric Association. (2000). *Diagnostic and statistical manual of mental disorders-IV* (4th ed.). Washington, DC: Author.

Attneave, C. (1982). American Indians and Alaska Native families: Emigrants in their own homeland. In M. McGoldrick, J. Pearce, & J. Giordano (Eds.), *Ethnicity and family therapy* (pp. 55–83). New York: Guilford Press.

Balkin, J. M. (2002). *The laws of change: I' Ching and the philosophy of life.* Toronto: Random House.

Barks, C. (1977). *The essential Rumi.* San Francisco: Harper.

Baynes, F. C. (l950). *The I' Ching or book of changes.* Princeton, NJ: Bollingen Press.

Bible. (2001). *New Oxford Annotated Bible.* Oxford & New York: Oxford University Press.

Biko, S. (1970). Cry freedom project options [Online]. Available at www.Ffjh. davis. k12.ut.us/CARPER/CRYFREE.html

Brave Heart, M. (1998). The return to the sacred path: Healing the historical trauma and historical unresolved grief response among the Lakota through a psycho-educational group intervention. *Smith College Studies in Social Work, 68,* 287–305.

Brave Heart, M. (1999). Oyate Ptayela: Rebuilding the Lakota Nation through addressing historical trauma among Lakota parents. *Journal of Human Behavior in the Social Environment, 2,* 109–126.

Brave Heart-Yellowhorse, M. (2000). Wakiksuyapi: Carrying the historical trauma of the Lakota. *Tulane Studies in Social Welfare, 21–22,* 245–266.

Brave Heart-Yellowhorse, M. (2003). The historical trauma response among Natives and its relationship with substance abuse: A Lakota illustration. *Journal of Psychoactive Drugs, 35*(1), 7–13.

Butz, M. R. (1993). The vampire as a metaphor for working with abuse. *Journal of Orthopsychiatry, 63*(2), 426–431.

Churchill, W. (1998). *A little matter of genocide.* San Francisco: Citylight Books.

Clements, F. E. (1932). Primitive concepts of disease. *University of California Publications in Archeology and Ethnography, 32,* 85–252.

Curry, A. (1972). *Bringing forth forms.* Paradise, CA: Dustbooks.

Danieli, Y. (1998). *International handbook of multigenerational legacies of trauma.* New York: Plenum Press.

Duran, E. (2000). *Buddha in redface.* Lincoln, NE: IUniverse.

Duran, E., & Duran, B. (1995). *Native American postcolonial psychology.* Albany: State

University of New York Press.

Duran, E., Duran, B., Yellowhorse, M., & Yellowhorse, S. (1998). Healing the American Indian soul wound. In Y. Danieli (Ed.), *International handbook of multigenerational legacies of trauma* (pp. 341–354). New York: Plenum Press.

Epstein, H. (1979). *Children of the Holocaust.* New York: Putman.

Erickson, E. (1980). *Identity and the life cycle.* New York: Norton.

Fannon, F. (1963). *The wretched of the Earth.* New York: Grove Press.

Foucault, M. (1967). *Madness and civilization.* London: Tavistock.

Frankl, V. (1959). *Man's search for meaning.* Boston: Beacon Press.

Freire, P. (1990). *Pedagogy of the oppressed.* New York: Continuum Press.

French, L. (2002). *Counseling American Indians.* Lanham, MD: Rowman & Littlefield.

Freud, A. (1967). *Ego and the mechanisms of defense.* Guilford, CT: International Universities Press. (Original work published 1912)

Freud, S. (1913). On beginning the treatment. In J. Strachey (Ed. & Trans.), *The standard edition of the complete psychological works of Sigmund Freud* (Vol. 12, pp. 14–144). London: Hogarth Press.

Freud, S. (1980). *The interpretation of dreams.* London: Avon Press. (Original work published 1900)

Goetz, D., & Morley, S. G. (1953). *Popol Vuh: The sacred book of the ancient Quiche Maya.* Norman: University of Oklahoma Press.

Gould, S. J. (1981). *The mismeasure of man.* New York: Norton.

Jung, C. G. (1954). *The practice of psychotherapy.* Princeton, NJ: Bollingen Press.

Jung, C. G. (1971). *Psychological types.* Princeton, NJ: Bollingen Press.

Jung, C. G. (1977). *The practice of psychotherapy.* Princeton, NJ: Bollingen Press.

Jung, C. G. (l988). *Nietzsche's Zarathustra* (J. Jarrett, Trans. & Ed.). Princeton, NJ: Bollingen Press.

Levi-Strauss, C. (1958). *Anthropologie structurals.* Paris: Library Press.

Lowrey, L. (1983). Bridging a culture in counseling. *Journal of Applied Rehabilitation Counseling, 14,* 69–73.

Manson, S. (2004). *Meeting the mental health needs of American Indians and Alaska Natives* (Report to the National Technical Assistance Center). Washington, DC: U.S. Department of Health and Human Services.

Marshall, J. M. (2004). *The journey of Crazy Horse.* New York: Viking.

Miller, D. (1983). The Native American family: The urban way. In E. Corfman (Ed.), *Families today* (pp. 441–484). Washington, DC: U.S. Government Printing Office.

Neihart, J. (1959). *Black Elk speaks.* New York: Simon & Schuster.

Ryan, R. (Director/Producer). (2002). *The healing road* [Film]. Berkeley: Rayen Productions.

Shore, J. H. (1988). Introduction. *American Indian and Alaskan Native Mental Health Research, 1,* 3–4.

Shoshan, T. (1989). Mourning and longing from generation to generation. *American Journal of Psychotherapy, 43*(2), 193–207.

Sinha, D. (1984). Psychology in the context of third world development. *International Journal of Psychology,* 17–29.

Solomon, Z., Kotter, M., & Mikulincer, M. (1988). Combat-related posttraumatic stress disorder among second-generation Holocaust survivors: Preliminary findings. *American Journal of Psychiatry, 145*(7), 865–868.

Spivak, G. (1990). Can the subaltern speak? In C. Grossberg & N. L. Grossberg (Eds.), *Marxism and the interpretation of culture* (pp. 271–313). Urbana: University of Illinois Press.

Sue, D. W., & Sue, D. (1990). *Counseling the culturally different* (2nd ed.). New York: Wiley.

Thornton, R. (1987). *American Indian Holocaust and survival: A population history since 1492.* Tulsa: University of Oklahoma Press.

Trimble, J. E., & LaFromboise, T. (1985). American Indians and the counseling process: Culture adaptation and style. In P. B. Pedersen (Ed.), *Handbook of cross-cultural counseling and therapy* (pp. 127–134). Westport, CT: Greenwood Press.

Trungpa, C. (1975). *The Tibetan Book of the Dead.* Boulder, CO: Shambala Press.

Villanueva, M. (2003). Posttraumatic stress disorder, alcohol, and tribes: Obstacles to research. *Alcoholism: Clinical and Experimental Research, 27*(8), 1374–1380.

W., Bill. (2005). *Alcoholics Anonymous big book* (4th ed.). A.A. World-Services.

Whitbeck, L., Adams, G., Hoyt, D., & Xiaojin, C. (2004). Conceptualizing and measuring historical trauma among American Indian people. *American Journal of Community Psychology, 33*(3–4), 119–130.

Zitgow, D., & Estes, G. (1981, April). The heritage consistency continuum in counseling Native American children. In *American Indian issues in higher education* (pp. 133-139). Spring Conference on Contemporary American Issues, Denver.

Index

Aboriginals. *See* Native Americans/ Original Peoples
Acculturation assessment, 4, 40, 47, 81, 84
Adams, G., 17
Addiction. *See also* Alcoholism
  as characteristic of intelligent being, 61–62
  as spiritual disorder, 62–64
Adler, G., 62–63
African American slavery, ix
Alcoholics Anonymous, 62–68, 72–73
Alcoholism, ix, 3–4, 25, 60–78
  addiction as spiritual disorder, 62–64
  alcohol as spirit and, 60–63, 65–76, 114
  case studies on, 66–77
  in case study on violence, 50–56
  with depression and anxiety, 83
  naming ceremony for, 64–66
  sobriety movement, 25, 62–68, 72–73
  splitting process and, 30
American Indians. *See* Native Americans/ Original Peoples
American Psychiatric Association, 1–2, 19
Animus, 88
Anxiety. *See* Depression and anxiety
Archetypes, nature of, 88
Assimilation, degree of, 3
Attneave, Carolyn, 4
Authority, language of, 40

Balkin, J. M., 133
Barks, C., 29
Baynes, F. C., 96–97
Bible, 71–72
Biko, Steven, 13
Black Elk, 45–46
Blaming the victim, 20, 21, 30–31
Boarding school era, 26, 52–53, 94, 117

Brave Heart, M., 16
Brave Heart-Yellowhorse, M., 16
Buddha, 109
Buddha in Redface (E. Duran), 60
Butz, Michael R., 17–18

Cartesian split, ix, 5, 10, 19
Case studies
  on alcoholism, 66–77
  on depression and anxiety, 83–111
  on dream interpretation in groups, 76–77
  on feeling function, 56–58
  purpose of, 10
  on violence, 50–56
Centering process, 45–46
Change agents, in community intervention, 118
Charting procedures, 36
Christian tradition, 47, 51, 71–72, 81, 119–121
Churchill, W., 22
Clements, Frank E., 5–6, 29–30, 32
Client-centered therapy, 4, 45
Clinical racism, 35–38
  agency/director characteristics and, 36–38
  as term, 36
Clinical supervision, 124–132
  challenges of, 124–125
  sample supervisory dialogue, 125–131
Cognitive therapies, 19–20
Colonial processes
  boarding school era and, 26, 52–53, 94, 117
  bureaucratic violence of, 25–26
  decolonization and, 14, 68–69
  dominant culture and, 34–35
  impact of, 14, 116

About the Author

Eduardo Duran has been working in Indian country all of his professional career. During that time he has helped to establish Tribal-based as well as Urban behavioral health systems. *Healing the Soul Wound* is based on the clinical experience accumulated over more than 2 decades of clinical work. Duran has also taught graduate school and has published several papers in professional journals and magazines. He continues to lecture in this country and in international settings.

The author's training is comprised of Western approaches as well as training with Native healers and community. Many of the clinical strategies delineated in this book are an amalgamation of these teachings and can be traced to the teachings of his Root Teacher, Tarrence. Therefore, this book is the clinical application of the ideas described in his previous book, *Buddha in Redface*, which is a narrative of Duran's experiences with his teacher. Presently, Duran is director of health and wellness for the United Auburn Indian community. He lives in the forest east of Colfax, California.